Orphan

Orphan

A True Story of Abandonment, Abuse, and Redemption

Roger Dean Kiser, Sr.

Adams Media Corporation
Holbrook, Massachusetts

Published by
Adams Media Corporation
260 Center Street
Holbrook, MA 02343
www.adamsmedia.com

ISBN: 1-58062-448-0

Printed in Canada.

J I H G F E D C B

Library of Congress Cataloging-in-Publication data
available upon request from the publisher.

This book is available at quantity discounts for bulk purchases.
For information, call 1-800-872-5627.

Everything in this book is true. I was there and this is how it happened. But I have changed most of the names—of the institutions where I lived, their staff members, my fellow orphans, and even my own birth mother and stepfather. Some of the names are changed on the advice of lawyers because these people engaged in cruel behavior. I have also changed the names of my fellow orphans and the institutions in order to protect the privacy of my fellow orphans. However, I have kept the real names of many of the people who were kind to me at times when kindness was hard to come by.

This is the true story of Roger Dean Kiser, Sr., an orphan, who was physically, mentally, and sexually abused by The Children's Association, the Institute for Young Men, Florida at Marianna, and the State of Florida. His poignant messages are sharp, sad, and abusive; they have a deep effect on the feelings, yet sometimes are humorous. His is a heartfelt message that should be read by all who truly love children.

—Judith Ann Kiser

DEDICATION

To all the orphans of the world—not because of all the beatings that they endured, or the abuse, or the hunger, or the slaps, or the yells, or the kicks, or the burns—but because of all those heartbreaking hours that they spent all alone between the beatings, the abuse, the hunger, the slaps, the yells, the kicks, and the burns.

To Larry Eugene Peterson, for writing the song "A Boy I Used to Know," which gave me the strength and courage to tell my story. After Larry's death, I vowed to him that my story, and his story, and those of other unwanted children must be told.

To my orphan brother, Wayne Evers, who for years cried along with me and who also suffered the ungodly experiences described in this book. We suffered these injustices simply because we were innocent, unloved, and unwanted children, children who had never hurt anyone.

A Boy I Used to Know

I'm a time traveler, I travel back in time.
Never to the future for I'm afraid of what I'll find.
I travel back in time, to a time long ago.
I travel back to see a boy I used to know.
He's a lonely boy, a lost orphan boy.
He walks all alone, no one to call his own.
No one to care, no one's love to share.
He walks all alone, no one to call his own.
I'm a time traveler, I travel back in time.
Never to the future for I'm afraid of what I'll find.
I travel back in time, to a time long ago.
I travel back to see a boy I used to know.
I've seen so many tears, all through the years.
There was no one to hold him, nor to wipe away the tears.
It hurt so much to see the boy cry.
It hurt so much, I wanted to die.
I'm a time traveler, I travel back in time.
Never to the future for I'm afraid of what I'll find.
I travel back in time, to a time long ago.
I travel back to see a boy I used to know.

CONTENTS

ACKNOWLEDGMENTS

THE JOURNEY TO WRITE AND PUBLISH THIS BOOK HAS not been an easy one. But I have to say that I have met some very nice people along the way. People who have been selfless and given freely of themselves. My orphan brothers and sister: Chuck Reynolds, Wayne Evers, Charles Nichols, Larry Peterson, and Margaret Baylor, whose personal stories gave me the strength and courage to stand up and tell the world the truth about some of America's orphanages. Kathy Belew, who worked hundreds of hours for free designing and developing my Web site. Without Kathy's help, my stories would never have been seen or discovered in the first place. To my friend Lee Simonson and his entire staff at Heartwarmers4u.com, who published many of my stories, though criticism may have lurked over the horizon. In addition, I have to mention the thousands of Heartwarmer4u readers who lifted my spirits with their thousands of e-mails over the years. Thanks to Edward Asner and Skip Press, who headed me in the right direction because they felt that I had a message that the world needed to hear.

A special thanks to all my friends at Sonny's Bar BQ Restaurant for their support.

A publishing company and the staff assigned to convey to the world the type of stories that I had to tell must put their own hearts into the book or the story loses its feeling and it dies before the printing process ever begins. I wish to thank Paula Munier Lee (who got me into the batter's box), Dawn C. Thompson (thank you for being so kind and considerate and for keeping the ball rolling), Erika Heilman, Paul Beatrice (WOW! A perfect job big guy. I am very proud of that book cover), Sue Beale and her production team, Edward Walters, and Bob Adams. Thank you all for keeping the spirit of this book alive through this long, hard process. I hope that putting this book together was just more than a job for all of you. I want each and every one of you to share the wonderful feeling of accomplishment and pride that I feel inside myself, and all because of you. The thoughts, those ideas, that word, that picture, and even that suggestion are pieces of each of you that will live in this book forever.

I wish to thank those who stood beside me. My wife, Judy; my son, Roger, and my daughter-in-law, Jamie; my friends Craig and Pam Johnson, R. L. and Doris Hall, who always patted me on the back every time they saw me on the street; and my special friend Sharen Jackson, who spent countless hours proofreading my stories.

Of course my granddaughter, Chelsey, who complained that her papa never had time to play with her because he was always writing something at the computer.

INTRODUCTION

FIRST, PLEASE UNDERSTAND THAT I REALIZE THERE ARE good people and bad people everywhere. These stories are in no way intended to generalize about humankind or to say that all things done for children through agencies of protective services are bad. In fact, I know of many children who have been helped and even saved by protective services.

My hope is that by reading these stories, people will come to understand what horrible things *can* happen to children while in the custody of the county, state, or government agencies and that more checks and balances and monitoring will be done as a result of revealing such atrocities. It is important to realize that children must be given the opportunity to voice their concerns, away from their custodians and without the threat of punishment or physical and emotional harm. Just ask the children. These stories will show that children do have feelings.

I tell these stories of my life as a young boy—in an orphanage, reform school, juvenile hall, and out on my own at times—not out of self-pity or because I want anyone to feel sorry for me. I have written them, to the best of my ability, from a child's point of view so that the world will know and understand what a child secretly thinks and feels when he or she is abused and is afraid to speak out about it.

It has not been easy exposing the inner thoughts of an orphan, an abused child, a juvenile delinquent, a criminal, an ex-con, and now a self-rehabilitated grandfather, who has reformed himself and now lives in "the real society." Nor has it been easy disclosing my private life, my personal thoughts, my hatreds, and my private sexual issues. However, because of our changing world and the ever-increasing danger that our children face, including school shootings and domestic problems, the experiences of people such as myself, who are considered and labeled dysfunctional individuals, must be written about, looked at, studied, and evaluated. It can only help to look at the problems squarely and to raise the public consciousness in the process.

What I wish for you to remember is that the pain and sadness you will no doubt feel while reading these stories will disappear for you within a minute, an hour, a day, or a week. You will once again return to your normal life, with your normal feelings. The orphan shall forever remain in that state of sadness and loneliness. This sadness and suffering has become who I am as a person. It is the person I wake up with every morning of my life. It is impossible for the orphan to forget sadness or loneliness because it is all he or she knows, all he or she has been taught from an early age. Those of you who have lost a mother or a father (or both) might be able to somewhat understand. It is a sadness that tears your heart out at the core. But, if you've been raised by loving relatives, you may find a way to overcome your sadness with the good memories of all the devotion, guidance, tenderness, hugs, and most of all the love that you received from your lost parent. You are able to "get over it" because you will have a memory of the good things to carry you onward and to hold on to. The orphan has none of these things. There are no good, kind, or loving things for him or her to remember. So when there is no love to remember, the only thing left is the hate.

It is not the physical pain that endangers orphans the most. It is the mental pain caused by stress from years and years of being neglected, pushed aside, disregarded, unloved, and made to feel undeserving, and in almost all cases, made to feel like a possession rather than an equal human being. Even more, it is the lack of "unconditional love," the right to be accepted, as a child, and to be loved, as a child, no matter what you do that is the most wounding.

Despite all of this, the orphan can succeed in life—but only because he learns to rule and structure his life with his thought processes rather than with his emotional processes. You do this purely as a form of survival, closing out the pain and going forward as best you can. Although the experiences I describe here are forever with me, I have been able to move on with my life and now have a wife, four children, and eight grandchildren. I have learned much from the pain that I have suffered. I have lived on both the good side and the bad side of the fence and sincerely hope that the world can learn something through what I have written.

The content of these stories may be difficult for you to read; they reveal the whole, horrible truth about the cruelty, despair, and loneliness that exist in certain orphanages in the United States, as well as other countries of the world. They are intended to educate people with the hope of improving the lives of the innocent, unfortunate souls who do not have someone of their own to care for them. The time has finally come to speak for the good of all. This piece of hope is all that I have left to offer to the world, the hope of making it a better place.

Roger Dean Kiser, Sr.

❖ *Before* ❖

E VEN TO THIS DAY, I AM NOT SURE WHAT EFFECT THIS experience, one of my earliest memories, has had on my life. I do know, however, that I am haunted by the memory of it, somewhere in my mind. As I was only about four years old, I cannot remember many of the details associated with the gruesome event. In fact, the only detail that I clearly recall is at one point being dragged around the living room by some man with a telephone cord wrapped around my small neck. I decided to ask Mr. Steven Avery of White Oak, Georgia, to tell me what he knew of this event.

Apparently, Mr. Avery was married to my mother about that time, and they had a child together, my half-sister Linda. As the story goes, my mother, Patricia, was expecting another baby. Mr. Avery was in the United States Navy and could not make it back in time for the delivery. Besides, he had heard that Patricia was dating several other men, so Mr. Avery could not be sure that this baby was his anyway. His position was that he would pay the hospital bill under his military insurance and then let Patricia continue on with her life just as she had always done in the past. His theory is most likely true. To this day, I have no idea who my own father is.

Several months after the baby was born, the next-door neighbors telephoned the police department. They told the police that there were several children in the house next door and that no adults had been seen at the residence for more than a week. When the police arrived, all the doors and windows were locked, so they broke out a window in the kitchen. They found Linda sitting in the corner of the kitchen, crying, with human waste smeared all over herself. When they walked into the living room, the police found me sitting in the middle of the floor, holding a dead baby and trying to feed it corn flakes. The only other food found in the house was several cans of beans, which had all been smashed and dented.

The police concluded that either Linda or I had beaten the cans against the door jam in order to try to get to the food contained within. They also concluded that Linda and I had survived nearly an entire week on a large bowl of dog food that had been left beneath the kitchen table, and that we had drunk water from the toilet because we could not reach any of the faucets.

As I was about four years old, that would have made Linda about three. The baby, a boy, had been only a few months old.

After the police found Linda and I at the house with the dead baby, we were kept in a home for three days until Steven Avery could be located. He took us from California to Lakeland, Florida, by train to stay with his parents.

They wanted to get rid of me, as Steven had taken me from California from my mother, who had total custody. She was threatening Steven's parents for taking me and the grandparents told her that I was not with them. They wanted to have the public schoolteacher (Mrs. Harrell) say that I was retarded and then they could secretly place/hide me in the Sunnyland Training Center for Children. That way my mother would never know that Steven had taken me, and he would not get into legal trouble. ❖

SHORTLY AFTER THE POLICE FOUND US IN THE KITCHEN, WE were placed with Mr. Avery's parents. Other than in the orphanage, I cannot remember being kicked, slapped, or beaten as much as I was by my stepgrandparents. Almost every night, I remember one of them coming into my bedroom with a bag over his or her head, with a light inside, trying to scare me and saying over and over, "Youuuuuu are CRAZYYYYYYY, Youuuuuu are CRAZYYYYYYY." I would sit in the living room and hear my stepgrandparents telling everyone who came to their house that I was mentally retarded and that they wanted to put me in a home for mentally retarded children. But they told people that they did not know how to do it legally, as I was not related to them, and that they could not afford to send me away.

I vaguely remember my grandma taking me across the street to the Dixieland Elementary School in Lakeland, Florida, to talk with a teacher. I remember them talking with one another and I overheard my grandma telling the teacher, "Now, Mrs. Harrell, you don't have to teach this child to read. He is feeble-minded and all I want you to do is sign a paper saying that he can't learn, and we will put him in the Sunnyland Training Center."

After my grandma left the school, I remember Mrs. Harrell putting her arm around me and saying that she was going to teach me to read even if it killed her. "That really gets my back up," she said as she walked back to her desk to get the papers to give me an IQ test. The test said to move the marker down to the thing that makes music and I didn't know what it was, so I asked Mrs. Harrell. She told me that it was a test and that she could not help me, but she told me that she would show me the answer after the test was over. After I had finished, she showed me that the answer was a grand piano. I looked at her and said, "Just how do you expect me to know that when I have never seen one?" Mrs. Harrell grabbed me out of my chair, picked me up, and hugged me as hard as she could. She then looked at me and said, "Not only are you not retarded, you are very, very smart."

The next day Mrs. Harrell started teaching me to read and within a week she said I was "reading handily." She let me take a book home from school because I liked to read, and when my grandma found out that I could read, she grabbed me by the shirt and dragged me over to the school building. I was screaming and my legs were all cut up and bleeding from her dragging me across the pavement. Grandma started yelling at all the teachers and at Mrs. Harrell, who just smiled at me. "You just hate that boy, don't you?" hollered Mrs. Harrell, as she grabbed me by the hand. "He will not be back to this damn school," yelled Grandma, as she snatched me back from Mrs. Harrell. When we got back over to the house, Grandma beat me with a fly swatter and the leather strap and made me go to bed. The next morning I was looking out the front door at all the children going into the schoolhouse. I wanted to see my friend, Mrs. Harrell, because she liked me and I liked her.

I crossed the street to play on the merry-go-round in the schoolyard. My grandma came running across the street with a leather strap and began hitting me across the face and back. I remember running from her and trying to crawl on my hands and knees to get under the steel bars of the merry-go-round to stop the strap from hitting me.

She finally stopped the merry-go-round and my grandpa came over and grabbed me by the ear and picked me up. Grandma came around and began hitting me with the leather strap. I tried to run, but Grandpa would not let go of my ear. They beat me from the school grounds to the house across the street. Two or three ladies from the school came running out and started yelling at my grandma to stop beating on me before she killed me. One of the women called my grandma "a snake" and told her she was going to call the police and then ran back toward the school.

After the three of us got inside of the house, Grandma told my grandpa to get my pants off because I had wet on myself during the beating. He grabbed me and started ripping my little pants off. As he did, he yelled at Granny to bring the leather strap because I had also messed on myself. They hit me several times across the back of the head. Then Grandma took the pants and started rubbing the mess into my face. They took me over to the sink and washed me off. Then I was taken out on the pickle porch and hosed off with cold water.

About an hour later the police showed up and began to question the two about what the school had reported. The police told them that they wanted to see me to make sure that I was all right. My granny told the policeman that I was asleep and asked if they could come back later.

One of the police officers walked in and out of each of the bedrooms, trying to find me, but I was nowhere in the house. When the policeman finally found me, I was standing out in the back yard, naked, with black and blue marks all over my body and both of my little arms stretched upward toward the sky— holding my pants up to the sun so they would dry. ❖

❖ *During* ❖

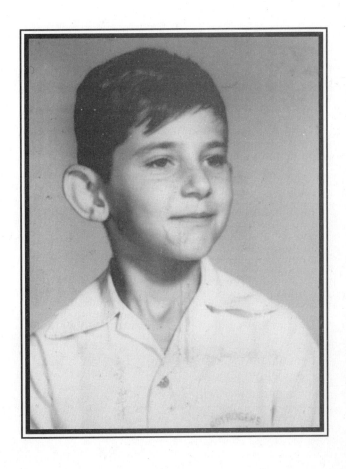

I AM NOT SURE HOW LONG I WAS IN THE NANCY SPARROW orphanage in Lakeland, Florida, after I was taken away from my grandma and grandpa's house. I was in and out of the hospital so many times that I don't remember much of anything. I do remember my grandma and grandpa coming to the orphanage to see me, just one time, but the orphanage lady ran them off for some reason. After Grandma and Grandpa came to see me, the orphanage lady took me to see a doctor because I could not speak for almost a month. No matter how hard I tried, no words would come out of my mouth, even when I tried real hard to talk to the lady at the hospital office.

One day after I returned from the hospital, I was sitting on the top step when a lady at the orphanage started yelling at me. She said the other children were all going swimming somewhere and that I had to go with them. I was too afraid to leave the building or to go outside. She told me that if I did not get up and go with them that none of the other children would be allowed to go swimming. But I just couldn't get up enough nerve to go outside. The next day I would not even go outside of my room, so I was pulled down the steps by my legs by two women and dragged out of the building and carried to a waiting car. The woman driving the car laughed at me and told me to stop crying.

We drove for miles and miles and I asked her if she was taking me to see my grandma and grandpa. She told me that she and I "were going to see America together." After we drove for a long time, she asked me if I liked fruit. I did not say anything to her at all because she laughed at me as I was being dragged down the stairs, so in my mind she was a bad person. Then she pulled over to this little fruit stand beside the road and asked me to wait in the car. I looked over at the fruit stand and I saw these little American flags in a bucket, so I got out of the car and picked one up and started waving it all around. "I'm going to see America," I kept telling everyone who walked by. This man took the flag from my hand and put it back into the bucket and picked up a big American flag, almost as big as I was, and asked the lady selling the flags how much it was. She told him what it cost and he reached into his pocket, took out some money, and paid her for the flag. Then, he handed me the great big flag and said, "Welcome to America, little boy."

We continued our drive for what seemed like a long, long time. We finally turned into these large, white gates with high metal fences all around and stopped in front of a building. A man and woman came walking up to the car and asked me to get out. The man took my flag and threw it on the ground. I ran over and picked it up as fast as I could and shook it off. I told him that the American flag was never supposed to touch the ground and now I would have to burn it like the rule says.

He once again snatched the flag from my hand and broke the stick in half and threw it to the ground.

I guess I had seen a piece of America when our journey was finally over. Little did I know that America had its own form of concentration camps. ❖

I WAS A VERY SCARED LITTLE BOY WHEN I WAS TRANSFERRED from the Nancy Sparrow orphanage to The Children's Association in Jacksonville, Florida. Lots of buildings. Lots of trees and bushes. Lots of chain-link fences, too—great big fences with great big white gates.

This mean-looking old woman came over to me when I arrived. She told a bigger boy to take the "little bastard" over to the boys' building and "give the little bastard a bath." The bigger boy grabbed me by the hand and led me over to a large, white building. In the back of the building there was a room that had a large cement sink with two sides. He placed me in the sink and ran some hot water. He washed me for several minutes.

The old woman came in. He began to tell her that he could not get my elbows clean. She left the room and came back with two gallons of bleach, which they dumped onto my head. I remember starting to cry as the bleach was burning my eyes. After several minutes my whole body was burning, and I was turning red. I was screaming and yelling at the top of my voice. The old lady grabbed me by the top of the head and tried to push me down underneath the water and bleach. I do not remember much after that, except waking up in the hospital. Little did I realize that this would be the beginning of many incidents after which I ended up in bad shape. ❖

THERE WAS A TIME IN MY LIFE WHEN BEAUTY MEANT something to me. I guess that would have been when I was about six years old, just several months before I became a wise old man.

I would get up every morning at the orphanage, make my bed just like the little soldier that I had become, and then I would get into one of the two straight lines and march to breakfast with the other twenty or thirty boys who also lived in my dormitory.

After breakfast one Saturday morning, I returned to the dormitory and saw the house parent chasing the beautiful monarch butterflies that lived by the hundreds in the azalea bushes planted all around the orphanage.

I carefully watched as he caught these beautiful creatures, one after the other, and then took them from the net and stuck straight pins through their head and wings, pinning them onto a heavy cardboard sheet.

How cruel it was to kill something of such beauty, I thought. I had walked many times out into the bushes, all by myself, just so the butterflies could land on my head, face, and hands so I could admire their beauty up close.

When the telephone rang, the house parent laid the large sheet of cardboard down on the back cement step and went inside to answer the phone. I walked up to the cardboard and looked at the butterfly he had just pinned down. It was still moving about, so I reached down and touched it on the wing, causing one of the pins to fall out. It started flapping around and around trying to get away, but it was still pinned by the other wing with another straight pin. Finally its wing broke off and the butterfly fell to the ground and just quivered. I picked up the torn wing and the butterfly and spit on its wing and tried to get it to stick back on so it could fly away and be free before the house parent came back. But the wing would not stay on.

The next thing I knew, the house parent came walking back out of the back door by the garbage room and started yelling at me. I told him that I didn't do anything, but he didn't believe me. He picked up the cardboard paper and started hitting me on the top of the head. There were all kinds of butterfly pieces going everywhere. He threw the cardboard down on the ground and told me to pick it up and put it in the garbage can inside the back room of the dormitory and then he left.

I sat there in the dirt for the longest time, trying to fit all the butterfly pieces back together so I could bury them whole, but it was too hard to do. So I prayed for them and then I put them in an old, torn-up shoebox, and I buried them in the bottom of the fort that I had built in the ground out by the large bamboos, near the blackberry bushes.

Every year after that when the butterflies would return to the orphanage and try to land on me, I would try and shoo them away because they did not know that the orphanage was a bad place to die. ❖

I T WAS NOVEMBER 20, 1951, WHICH WAS MY SIXTH
birthday, and the house parent was going to do something
special for me because I had cleaned all the bathroom
floors, showers, sinks, and toilets, upstairs and downstairs. I
spent the entire day cleaning the bathrooms really good and
extra special clean because the matron told me she would bake
me a cake and I could give all the boys a piece while we watched
television later that evening. I was really very happy and excited
about that, because I could do something nice for all the boys
and everyone would like me and we could all have a good time.

About six o'clock all the boys took their showers and gathered
in the television room and each boy was asked to stand and say
one of the Ten Commandments. When Owen Hunt was called
upon, he stood up and said, "Thou shalt not spit," and everyone
just about died laughing because Owen was only three years old
and did not know the Ten Commandments. I laughed real hard,
too, but I felt sorry for Owen. When I got my cake I was going
to give Owen the first piece and maybe the biggest piece of all.
We all watched television and talked and I told everyone about
my birthday cake and that it would be ready soon.

Then the house parent called me out of the television room and into the hallway and asked me if I had taken a piece of the cake. I told her that I had not touched the cake and that I had not even seen it. Then she took me into the kitchen and showed me the cake. There was a big piece torn out of the side and you could see where someone's fingers had grabbed the cake and torn it out. She took my hand and placed my fingers into the torn part of the cake and told me that they fit exactly into the finger slots. I just kept telling her over and over that I had not touched the cake.

She reached over and turned on the stove burner to allow it to get hot. Then she told me that if I did not tell her the truth that she would put my hand on the hot burner. I still continued to tell her that I had not taken any of the cake. She grabbed my arm and pulled me over by the stove and raised my hand toward the hot burner. I just kept trying to pull my hand and arm back from the burner and tried not to yell out so that the other boys would not hear me.

She reached over and turned the burner off and then touched my hand to the burner real fast and then told me to put it under the water faucet and then she rubbed butter on it. She told me to go back out into the television room and wait until she came out.

When I walked back out into the television room, all the boys knew that something was wrong but they did not say anything. About five minutes later the matron came out of the kitchen with a plate that had about fifteen small pieces of cake on it, each about the size of a quarter. She gave one piece of cake to each one of the boys, except me, and then she told all the boys that I had stolen most of the cake and that it was my fault that there was not more for them. None of the boys said anything to me, whatsoever. They just ate their cake and then they all went upstairs to bed. I had to stay downstairs and straighten up the television room and then I went to my bedroom.

When I got to my room there was a small piece of cake about half the size of a quarter lying on my pillow. I picked up the little piece of cake and I squeezed it because it was like a sponge, and then I ate it. Then I pulled my bedspread and sheet back and walked down to use the bathroom.

As I walked past Owen Hunt's room, he was sitting on the end of his bed sucking on his big toe. He pulled his toe out of his mouth and just smiled at me and then he reached over and picked up a small piece of cake about half the size of a quarter and put it in his mouth. Then he waved at me and stuck his big toe back into his mouth and began to suck again. I just smiled at him and then I hurried off to the bathroom, where I washed my mouth out real, real good with soap and water, and then I went to bed.

Thanks, Owen, wherever you are. ❖

I WAS SIX YEARS OLD WHEN I WET MY PANTS FOR THE FIRST time at school. Mainly because the orphanage had always forbidden us to use the bathroom except for when "they" thought it was necessary, I had become afraid to ask my first grade teacher to allow me to go and use the little boys' room. So I would just sit at my desk, shaking my legs back and forth, hoping that I could hold it until the bell rang.

But this time I was not so lucky; the pain was so severe and my little stomach hurt so badly that I tried to release just a little bit at a time so that the pain would go away and I would not start crying or become embarrassed in front of the entire class. But once it started coming out, I could not stop it, and the pain just got worse and worse. Several of the boys who were sitting behind me started laughing rather loudly, and then the entire classroom, realizing what had happened, also started laughing at me. The teacher motioned for me to come up in front of the classroom, handed me some newspaper, and told me to get down on my hands and knees and wipe up the water, which had run under several of the desks. I tried to laugh along with the other children, but I was so ashamed that I did not know what to do or say or how to act. So I just got on my knees and wiped very slowly, hoping that the bell would ring so that I would not have to look any of the other kids in the face.

Finally, the bell rang and the kids ran out for recess, calling me names as they went by my desk. The teacher stood over me and told me that I should be very ashamed of myself. She said that when the class resumed, I was to stand with my face in the corner for the remainder of the day. After I had cleaned up after myself, I walked out into the hallway and just stood there, too embarrassed to go out into the schoolyard with the other children.

When the school bell rang again and all the children started to file back into the classroom, I quickly ducked into the bathroom and hid in one of the stalls with my feet up on the toilet seat until everything became quiet. Then I ran out of the bathroom and down the long hallway and left the school building as quickly as I could. I knew that the teacher would call the orphanage and that I would be beaten or switched when I returned to the orphanage later that afternoon. So I decided I was going to run away and never come back.

As I walked around in the various neighborhoods, I happened across one house whose owners had left their garage door open. Leaning against the wall was a large BB rifle. I very slowly walked up to the building, looked around, and saw nobody. I then grabbed the rifle and ran as fast as I could back down Spring Park Road toward the school building. I stopped and crouched behind a large bush from where I could see the children moving around in my classroom. I opened the rifle to make sure there was plenty of ammunition and found it to be completely full. At that point I did not know what to do, where to go, or who to turn to. I only knew that I could never return to school or to the orphanage and that I wanted to get even with everyone for laughing at me.

I stood there for five minutes or so, just listening to the sounds of the passing cars and the birds singing in the large bush. Slowly I raised the rifle, looked down the barrel, and pointed the gun toward the school window where I scoped from child to child and from child to teacher. Then I directed my aim at several of the passing cars and the people driving them. Then I made my final decision, pointed the rifle toward the school building, and carefully placed my finger on the trigger. Holding my breath, I closed my eyes tightly. Slowly, I pulled the trigger until the long rifle jerked and fired with a bang. I just stood there for a moment, then let the rifle fall to the ground.

I felt something wet on my head, so I quickly took off my undershirt and wiped my face and eyes. I felt rather sick to my stomach, but after about a minute or so I pulled myself together and walked, very slowly, toward the large bush where I had been standing when I fired the weapon. I stood there, motionless, looking at what I had done. I saw all this blood. I could not believe that this was really happening or that I had done something this terrible. I reached out and touched the blood with my finger. I immediately dropped to my knees, then fell onto my face and stomach in the dirt, and just lay there crying. I rolled over onto my back and looked up at the beautiful blue sky and all the puffy white clouds. Then I slowly turned my head back down into the dirt. I lay there for the longest time just looking at the most beautiful orange and black colors lying next to my head. When I finally managed to get up enough nerve to touch the injured area, it was still very warm. I will never forget that limp, lifeless, broken neck and the warm, motionless body of the only thing—a red-winged blackbird—that I ever killed in my whole life.

I returned the BB gun to the house from where I had stolen it, and, yes, I did receive one hell of a beating when I returned to the orphanage later that evening. But it was a beating that this six-year-old killer did not mind taking. I just stood in the sewing room through the entire beating with my head hung in shame. As a child in the orphanage, I had always thought that there was nothing worse than being an orphan without parents or anyone to love me. Second to that would be having other children laugh at me because I had big ears, and, thirdly, having all the children laugh at me when I wet my pants at school because I was afraid to ask to go to the bathroom. When I returned to school the next day, the children were still laughing and making fun of me, but I had already learned a very important lesson about life. I now knew, in my heart, that there was an even more horrible feeling, far worse than not being loved as a little boy—which was to hold in the palm of my hand something warm, dead, and lifeless that I myself had selfishly killed with a gun. Something that was no longer to be, something that had only dropped by to sing to me because I was sad and all alone. In retrospect, the blackbird had perhaps given its own life to save the lives of others that I might have harmed that day and later on in my many moments of despair and anger. ❖

THE LEAVES FELL BY THE THOUSANDS AT THE ORPHANAGE. Each year, we children had to rake up truckloads upon truckloads of leaves and pine straw. Some days it was so hot that you could hardly breathe and the humidity in the air could almost choke you to death. But none of that mattered to the house parents who looked after us at the boys' dormitory. You raked and cleaned, rain or shine—it made no difference. And if it was winter time and there were no leaves or pine straw to rake up, you would rake the sandy dirt so that it always looked neat and clean.

You did not go to the bathroom nor did you ever go to get a drink of water without permission, even when you were allowed to play. No orphan was ever allowed to make such a decision on his own. In fact, we came to know that if you ever sneaked a drink of water or went to the toilet without asking that you would get the holy hell beat out of you.

Just when you felt you could not take it any more, one of the men in charge would call all the boys over and tell them to line up at the sulfur water spigot. Dean, Russell, Wayne, David, Jack, Emmett, Frank, and the other boys would run as fast as they could to get in line. After we had lined up and were standing at attention, the man would ask us what type of drink we wanted. Generally, Frank Snow would say, "I would like an Orange Crush, please." The man would laugh and then turn on the sulfur water faucet and tell him to drink all the Orange Crush that he wanted. God! I hated that sulfur water—it stunk so bad. But worse than that was the way they treated us, as if we were nothing more than dogs. Oh, how much a little hug and a kiss, once in a while, would have made that water taste so much better. Many of the boys didn't even realize what was happening or how badly the orphanage was treating us. We were treated like that for so long that we finally thought that it was normal and that all the children of the world were treated exactly like we were, even the ones who had real mommies and daddies. ❖

M Y HEART WAS BEATING NINETY MILES AN HOUR AS I walked as fast as a six-year-old boy could possibly walk. That two thousand yards from the boys' dormitory to the office of Mrs. Dalbert, the head matron of The Children's Association, was a very long distance to travel when one thought that he was in serious trouble and was going to get another beating.

We boys had worked very hard all day, raking bundles of pine straw and hauling endless armloads full of leaves into the azalea bushes, not even stopping for a drink of water. We hoped that if we worked hard enough, we'd be allowed to watch the little black-and-white television set that sat in the room next to the small kitchen.

As I arrived at her office, I opened the white door to the screened breezeway porch leading into the dining room area, which then led down a long, dark hallway going to the very secret place where Mrs. Dalbert lived, all by herself.

As I slowly closed the screen door behind me I heard a noise, which made me jump a little. I turned around to see Carol, the black maid for Mrs. Dalbert, come walking out of the infirmary and slam the door.

"How are you today, Mr. Roger?" she said. "I am fine, Miss Carol," I said back to her. I smiled at her and continued walking toward the dining room door. As I opened the door, I listened real close to see if I could hear anyone breathing before I entered the dining room. We always waited and listened before crossing a doorway, because if we entered with too much confidence, we were generally hit and knocked down, often beaten. I stood in the doorway for a moment, looking down the long, dark hallway leading to the room with the large piano in it. "Mrs. Dalbert, it is me, Roger. Mrs. Dalbert, it is me, Roger," I said softly. But no one answered.

I walked toward the hallway and stopped by the entrance, which led into the small bathroom that we used when we were eating in the large dining hall. "Mrs. Dalbert, I am here. It is me, Roger," I said again, a little louder. Still there was no answer. I slowly walked, using little timid steps, down the unlit hallway, and then stopped at the large doorway leading into the room with the big, shiny piano in it. "Hello," I said with my eyes open as wide as I could get them. But no one answered. I looked up at the far wall and saw a large picture in a wooden frame of a man they called "Daddy Fagg," the man who had started the orphanage many years before. He was looking right at me with a funny look on his face. I moved very slowly to the right, but his eyes followed me. I then moved back to the left, and his eyes followed me again. I walked on into the room to see if Mrs. Dalbert might be sitting in there in the big, soft chair. But she was not in there. As I started to turn around, I heard something crunch underneath my foot, so I looked down and saw that I had stepped on a Christmas tree light and it had broken.

I bent down and started picking up the broken glass and putting the little pieces into my shirt pocket when all of a sudden something knocked me to the floor. "Just what the damn hell do you think you are doing?" yelled Mrs. Dalbert, as she continued to hit me in the head with a wooden polo paddle. Over and over, she kept hitting me in the face and head. I scrambled onto my hands and knees and got beneath the grand piano so she could not hit me anymore. "Get your little ass out here right now!" she demanded, shaking the paddle at me. I climbed out from under the piano and stood before her. "BOINK," went the paddle as she hit me on the top of the head. "BOINK, BOINK," it went again as she hit me two more times. "Just what are you doing in the piano room?" she asked me. "Nothing. Just looking for you, Mother Dalbert," I said. "BOINK, BOINK," went the paddle again as it hit the top of my head. "I am not your damn mother, you little fart. I am Mother *Dalbert*." I just stood there not saying a word, too afraid to speak. "Do you understand that?" she said. "BOINK," went the paddle again. "Do you understand me, Roger?" she yelled. "Yes, Mother Dalbert," I said to her. Mrs. Dalbert told me to stand right where I was, and she turned around and walked down to the end of the long hallway and went into the secret closet by the bathroom.

Several minutes later she came back out and walked back down the hallway to where I was standing. She held out a large blue Christmas tree bulb and told me to place it in my mouth, which I did. She slapped me across the face with her hand and told me to spit it out into her hand. She took the bulb and wiped it off on my shirtsleeve and then placed the screwed-in part of the bulb in my mouth and told me to hold it between my teeth.

With the bulb in my mouth I followed her back down the hallway to the dining room, where she told me to wait for her on the porch. I walked out onto the porch where Miss Carol was still sweeping and cleaning. Miss Carol turned around and looked at me holding the blue Christmas bulb in my mouth, and started laughing. "What, or should I say who are we? The blue-nosed reindeer?" she said. I started laughing and could not stop. The next thing I knew Mrs. Dalbert shoved Carol against the infirmary doors, snatched the dustpan from her hand, and hit me in the face, knocking the bulb into my throat. When I fell to the floor, the bulb came out of my mouth and broke into pieces. "You clean up that mess and then get your black ass back into the infirmary," Mrs. Dalbert said to Miss Carol, as she turned and walked back down the long, dark hallway.

"It's okay, Mr. Roger. You'll be grown and out of here one day," said Miss Carol. Miss Carol and I cleaned up the blue Christmas bulb together and then I got my white ass back to the boys' dormitory as fast as I could. After that incident, I helped Miss Carol clean every chance I got until they finally sent me away to the reform school. I never saw Miss Carol again after that although I've often thought of her and how much I'd like to give her a great big hug. ❖

THREE TIMES A DAY, ALL OF US WOULD LINE UP TWO abreast and walk to the dining hall across the yard. We would wait on a large screened-in porch until all the other orphans arrived from the other cottages. We would then walk into the dining room and stand in front of our chairs until Mrs. Dalbert entered the room. She would walk to her place at the end table and bow her head. The entire room would then repeat, "Thank you, God, for this food, Amen." She would pick up a small bell and ring it. We would then all be seated and start to eat whatever was placed on the table.

Every morning we always got a little box of cereal. You could cut the box open and peel back the tin foil and neatly pour into a bowl that would hold milk. Real neat and tidy. But that was not the problem. Every morning the ritual was the same. You would shake your box, then cut open the package and pour, and sit the box back onto the table. Then all these small bugs would run out. There were hundreds of bugs in these packages—tiny little bugs, running everywhere, all over the table. This was sort of funny to us at first, but after a while lost its humor. Of course, we complained, but Mrs. Dalbert would tell us to shut our mouths and to be thankful that we had cereal at all.

Being the little troublemaker that I was, I decided to investigate the situation. I found out that the cereal had been donated to the orphanage by the United States Navy. I figured that this stuff had been at sea for several years and they needed to get rid of it. Of course, I started spreading the rumor that the little bugs were crabs, from the sailors. This did not sit well with Mrs. Dalbert, not to mention the cook, Charity.

Well, at least we got pancakes for the next few weeks or so. I should have realized right then that I should grow up to be a lawyer. ❖

E ACH YEAR AN ORGANIZATION OF MEN CAME TO THE Children's Association. All the boys and girls would get two dollars each. The men would take us in groups of five to downtown Jacksonville to do some Christmas shopping.

I remember going with this one gentleman three years in a row. He would take us shopping; then he would ask us if we wanted to go to the movies. I remember watching him really closely when we got to the theater. I watched him as he pulled out his wallet to pay for our tickets. He looked over at me and just smiled with his great big smile. During the movie he bought us all the popcorn and candy that we wanted.

I remember thinking how wonderful it was that someone would spend his own money on kids like us. We all laughed at the funny movie and had a really good time. The man would laugh really hard and then he would pat me on top of the head. Then he would laugh really hard again and reach over and tousle my hair. I would look at him, and he would just keep smiling with his great big wonderful smile.

That trip to the movies was the first time in my life that I ever felt as if someone really cared about me. It was a wonderful feeling that I have never forgotten, even to this day. I had never felt anything like that in my entire life.

I do not know if that man felt sorry for me or what, but I do know this: if I ever win the big lottery, that man will find out that he carried a million-dollar smile. I thank you, kind sir, for a fond memory that I still share with my children and grand-children, fifty years later. ❖

ONE DAY I WAS CHASING A BUTTERFLY IN THE AZALEA bushes at the orphanage when I heard someone yelling, "They are here! They are here!" All the boys started running as fast as they could toward the big white building where we all lived. I also started running, as fast as I could, wondering who and what the heck they were yelling about. All the boys ran up the stairs to their rooms and started digging out their Sunday best, which was not much at all. I walked to my room, took my Sunday clothes out of the closet and walked back down the hallway with them slung over my right shoulder. "Who is coming? Is it Santa Claus?" I said to one of the boys. "No, dummy," he hollered at me. "It's the mommies and daddies. Get dressed! Get dressed!" he yelled. I put on my Sunday clothes, wiped my shoes off on the corner of my bedspread, then walked out into the hallway, waiting to see what everyone else was going to do and where they were going in such an awful hurry.

It was like a mad house around there. There were boys running in and out of bedrooms and bathrooms and tripping all over one another. "Move it, you little brat," yelled one of the older boys as he ran into me, knocking me down. I stood up, brushed myself off, and then headed down the back stairway. "You had better comb your hair or you are not going to be picked by a mommy and daddy," said one of the boys. I slowly walked back up the stairs, went into the bathroom and looked at myself in the mirror. My hair was a mess and was sticking straight up in the back. Another boy came into the bathroom and I asked him what was going on. He told me that once in a while mommies and daddies came to the orphanage to buy kids and that they took them home, where they could live in their house and were given lots of toys and nice things. "But I don't want nice things, I just want a dog," I told him. "They have dogs too. Everyone who gets picked by the mommies and daddies gets a free dog and sometimes a baby!" he said. "I don't want no baby. I just want a dog," I replied.

I stood at the mirror for a long, long time trying to get my hair to lie down, but it just would not stay down. I knew right then that I would not get picked by the mommies and daddies and that I would not get a dog of my own. I tried and tried to make my hair stay down, but no matter what I did, it just wouldn't stay flat. I ran back to my bedroom and grabbed my toothpaste, put a little on my hand and rubbed my hands together, and then I rubbed the toothpaste through my hair and combed it. I looked into the mirror and to my surprise my hair was no longer sticking up. I ran out of the bathroom and down the stairs to catch up to the other boys who were now lined up on the front porch.

As I stood very proudly in line with my hair lying flat, the matron walked back and forth inspecting us, one at a time. When she got to me, she grabbed me by the arm and asked me what I had done to my hair. "Nothing," I told her. She jerked me by the arm, snatching me out of the lineup, and dragged me into the back room where there was a large cement sink. She ducked my head under the water faucet and washed my hair with the soap sock. Then she handed me a towel and told me to dry my hair. I dropped the towel because she was rushing me along and kept pushing me down the hallway with her hand in my back. When I bent over to pick up the towel, she kicked me in the rear end, saying, "If it is not one damn thing with you little bastards, it is another. I have a good mind to send you to your room." "I don't want to go to my room, I just want a dog," I told her.

She grabbed me by the arm again and herded me toward the front porch where the other boys were waiting. I saw Mrs. Dalbert, the head matron, walking down the road with a bunch of men and women. "Where are the mommies and daddies?" I asked one of the boys. "Right there, stupid," he said, as he pointed toward the group. "But you are not going to be picked 'cause you got big ears and your hair is sticking up," he said. I tried to slick my hair down again but it wouldn't stay. I lowered my hand and just stood there at attention, like the other boys.

The four or five couples walked up and down the line of kids, saying nothing. They just looked and smiled at each of us. Then this one woman stopped in front of me. I looked up at her and I said, "Do you have a dog for me?" "We don't have a dog, son," she told me. I looked at the boy next to me and said, "They don't have any dogs." "Do you brush your teeth every day?" she asked me. "I do with my finger," I said, very proudly. She bit her lip, turned, and walked away looking at the next boy in line.

I reached up and slicked my hair down again, getting ready for the next couple who was now walking down the line. But they passed me by without speaking at all as did the next and the next and the next one after that.

When I was about thirty years old, I went to the local dog pound to get a dog of my own. I walked up and down the line of cages looking at all those sad faces. Finally, I came across this one dog, whose hair was sticking up on her head and who had big ears. But I just did not have the heart to make a choice. It would hurt me too badly to take just one and leave all the others behind. So I left her there with the others, and I did not choose any of them at all. I hope that is the way it was when those mommies and daddies came to look at us kids—that it was just too sad for them to choose just one. ❖

EVERY DAY WE FILED PAST THE ORPHANAGE CLOTHING room, one at a time, and were handed clean clothes that we were to wear to school that day. There was no such thing as size, other than small or large. So color matching, tears, or holes really did not matter much to the house parents either.

I was tired of being made fun of at school by the other children because of the clothes I had to wear. Having big ears that stuck out was bad enough. But having to wear that kind of clothing day in and day out made it even worse on us orphan kids. I was so sick and tired of being dressed every day in clothes that were either two sizes too big or two sizes too small or full of holes.

One morning I marched down the stairs with the other boys and picked up my clothes and returned to my room to get dressed for school. After I got dressed I noticed that the pants that I had been given had a hole right in the front about the size of a quarter. If I had not been wearing underwear, you would have been able to see my thing-a-ma-bob.

I walked back down the stairs and saw that the clothing room door was closed and locked. I walked back upstairs to the matron's room and told her that my pants had a big hole right in the front. She told me that the hole was not big enough to worry about and that I would have to wear them anyway. I pulled my shirttail out of my pants and tried to cover the hole, but the shirt was so small that it would not reach the hole, much less cover it.

I walked to school with my Dick and Jane book over the hole and went directly to my second grade classroom and sat down at my desk, hoping that I would not have to get up all day long, not even to go to the bathroom.

When the class started, Mrs. Cherry started having the pupils come to the front of the classroom and read from the Dick and Jane book. When I was called upon, I told the teacher that I had not read the book and that someone else should read it. "Now, Roger, you know how to read and I want you to come up in front of the class and I want you to read your passage," said Mrs. Cherry. "I don't want to read and you can't make me. There is nobody who can make me," I told her.

I grabbed on to my desk and held on tightly as she walked toward me. Mrs. Cherry tried to force me out of the desk, but I would not budge an inch. She let go of me and walked back to the front of the classroom. "Now, Roger, if you do not come up here right now I will ask the entire classroom to remove you from your desk," she told me. I did not move an inch. "All right, class, let's see if we can show Roger who is the boss here," said Mrs. Cherry.

The entire classroom started coming toward me. I jumped up from my desk and just started swinging at anyone and everyone who came near me. I hit girls and I kicked boys and I hit or kicked them anywhere that I could.

Then I broke free, ran out of the classroom into the hallway, and just stood there crying, with my face stuck in the corner by the water fountain.

Mrs. Cherry came out into the hallway and asked me to sit down on the floor with her so she could talk to me. She asked me what was wrong and why I was acting like I was. I stood up and pointed to the big hole in my pants. She looked at me and then rubbed her hand down the side of my face. "I see," she said, as she wiped my eyes.

She got up and walked back into the classroom and then came back out holding her sweater in her hands. She told me to stand up and she wrapped her sweater around my waist so that it covered the hole in my pants. Then she took me to the principal's office and had me sit in a chair while she went in and talked with Mrs. Drayer.

A few minutes later I was in Mrs. Cherry's car and she and I were driving somewhere. We stopped at a store where she took me inside and bought me a new pair of Levi's and a brand new shirt—*and* some new socks without holes that didn't smell either.

There have been many terrible things that have happened to me during my lifetime, both as a child and as an adult. There has probably been only one act of kindness directed toward me for every one hundred unkind acts. But, believe it or not, somehow this has balanced the scale in my book. On that day, Mrs. Cherry showed me the power of kindness. ❖

I COULD HARDLY SLEEP THAT NIGHT, KNOWING THAT THE next day we had been invited to visit the Jacksonville Zoo.

I was seven years old and I had never been to the zoo before, but I knew what it was and I knew that they had all kinds of animals from all over the world. I sat up really late hiding in the bathroom, tracing pictures of all the animals out of a book that I was going to see the next day.

The next morning we ate our breakfast and then stood in line on the screened-in porch waiting to be loaded into the cars that had come to take us to the zoo. It was a long, long ride but that was okay with us because we did not get to go outside of the large orphanage fences except to go to school and church, and you did not get to go to church if you had been bad.

Of course, the matrons kept telling us to sit down and be quiet, that there was nothing to get excited about. "It is just a bunch of damn animals in a cage," they kept telling us. I don't think most of the boys cared anything about the animals. They were just glad to be outside of the fences and to get to see some of the other kids who lived in the outside world.

I was so excited when we finally pulled up and parked in the zoo's great big parking lot. You could smell all kinds of good stuff being cooked, like popcorn. One of the littler boys reached down and picked up half a candy apple and started eating it. "That's dirty," I told him as I took it away from him. "I want it, I want it," he kept saying. I took it over to the water fountain and washed it off. We had never had candy apples before and we probably never would so I took one bite and gave the rest to him.

As we entered the zoo, we were told to stay in one large group and to follow along closely as the matron took us down the long paths, from cage to cage, to see all the animals. I was amazed at all the different kinds of animals that they had and wondered how they could live here without dying if they were really from somewhere else on the earth.

Several of the other boys had run ahead and were all laughing at some of the bigger monkeys in one of the cages. When I got up to the cage I could see that one male monkey was doing something that was not very nice in front of ladies. One man told his wife, "I guess we came at the wrong time of the month," and then he laughed and they walked away from the monkey cage. I didn't know what he was talking about and just forgot about it.

The matron gathered us all together and then herded us over to a concession stand where they made us a hamburger and a drink, which I thought tasted real good. But some of the boys said it tasted like they made it from dead zoo animals, so I didn't eat any more, at least when they were looking at me.

When we got up to the elephant cage the big elephant was going to the bathroom, and it splattered everywhere, getting on this one man's shoes. All the boys were laughing and running around like crazy. The matron started hitting Nathan Lawrence on top of his head with her cotton candy and it stuck in his hair. Now everyone was really laughing, even the people who were not from the orphanage.

One matron was standing back from the rest of the group and kept scratching herself on her backside. She kept doing that over and over for a long time. Finally, several of the boys started talking about why she was doing that. She overheard them talking and told all of us to come over to her. She told us to mind our own business and keep our eyes straight ahead or that she would take us back to the home.

As we continued around the zoo we finally made it back to the big monkey cage. When we got there the matron started scratching herself again. When she did, the monkey started playing with his "bad thing" again, and all the boys started laughing uncontrollably. The matron started yelling at all of us to be quiet. I felt sorry for her, so I started acting like I was itching, too, so she would feel better. The boy next to me asked me what the big monkey was doing. I didn't know what to say except what the man had said earlier. But before I could answer the boy, the matron grabbed me by the hair and jerked me over to her. "What the hell is wrong with you? Are you mocking me?" she said. I was so scared that I did not know what to say, so I said, "I guess you came to the zoo at the wrong time of the month."

Well, if you don't think that a candy apple that the matron had in her hand can splinter into fifty million pieces and knock a big-eared orphan kid real stupid, you are badly mistaken. ❖

ALL OF US YOUNG, SCARED ORPHANS KNEW WE HAD TO face the daily ritual of marching to breakfast, dinner, and supper, day after day, week after week, month after month, and year after year. How horrible it was to have to wear a sheet wrapped around oneself like a diaper for having wet the bed, and then having to walk that long, horrible 2,000 yards to the dining room at the far end of the orphanage grounds.

I will never forget the house parents doing that to me. I will never forget the girls looking at me as we marched past their one-story dormitory. They spoke not a word as they stood in total silence with their eyes looking down toward the ground, nor was there a smile on any face or a giggle in any heart. Only the look of horror as they knew very well that this day would also come for one of them if they wet their beds, just as it had come for the poor topless, breastless little girl who had preceded me two weeks before.

If I have ever loved anyone, I will always love those children who bowed their heads with respect and reverence as I filed past as Caesar the bed wetter. ❖

I CAN STILL REMEMBER WHEN I SAW THE FIRST BOY HAULED off and dragged away from the orphanage by the police— one of my orphanage brothers taken away, never to be seen or heard from again.

I was playing in the dirt pile out by the orphanage heater room. There were large clumps of bamboo and I was hiding behind them when Eddie Gillman came running into the bamboo with two large men chasing him. One of the men grabbed him by the neck and threw him to the ground and started kicking him in the back. The other man grabbed Eddie by the hair and pulled him to his feet, then started dragging him by the hair toward the office building. One of Eddie's shoes came off and I ran over to pick it up.

When I got back into the bamboo area I noticed that there was something inside his shoe. I sat back down in the dirt and took everything out of the shoe, then threw the shoe against the tin heater building. There were several pennies, a nickel, a picture of an older woman, and three firecrackers.

About that time, one of the men, a police officer, came toward me and asked me where Eddie's shoe was. I told him that it was over by the tin building. The man walked over to the building and picked up the shoe and then came over to me and hit me in the leg real hard with the shoe, and told me to leave things alone that did not belong to me. I asked him what Eddie had done and where they were taking him. He said they were taking him to prison where he belonged and that he would take me, too, if I did not shut my mouth.

The man walked back toward the office, set the shoe on his car, and entered the orphanage office building. Several of the other boys came running over and asked me what was happening. I told them they were taking Eddie to the big prison and that was all I knew. Emmett (Eddie's brother) started to cry so I gave him the picture of the woman I had found in Eddie's shoe. Emmett told me that it was their mother and he ran off to his bedroom, which was against the rules. Then the office door opened and the two men came out with several women, and they put Eddie in the back of the police car.

Now, a whole bunch of the boys were crying and all of us just stood there until the car went out the big, white gate. I got up and followed the car toward the gate. As I watched the car turn the corner, I saw Eddie's shoe fall off the car. I ran over to the shoe, picked it up, and brought it back to the dirt pile.

I sat there for hours just looking at Eddie's shoe and I knew that he would never return, just like all the others who disappeared. I just kept wondering how a little boy could be taken to prison like that. But that is just the way it was in the orphanage. We all just sort of disappeared one at a time.

Eddie is now serving a life sentence in a Georgia prison. Not because of the two pennies, or the nickel, or the three firecrackers. I think it all started right there with the picture of that strange woman in Eddie's little shoe. ❖

ONE SATURDAY MORNING I WAS DOING CHORES, raking leaves with Dean Whitcomb and Wayne Evers. Dean grabbed a large armful of leaves and walked into a large section of azalea bushes to scatter them about. When I looked up, he had disappeared somewhere in the large rows of bushes. I told Wayne that I thought Dean was deliberately hiding from us, letting us do all the raking, and that we should discontinue raking until he returned.

We waited for about five minutes or so, but Dean never returned. So we started looking for him at the far end of the azalea bushes, working our way toward the opposite end about one hundred and fifty feet away. All of a sudden we heard someone screaming and yelling at the top of his voice. We ran out of the bushes and saw that it was Dean Whitcomb running around in circles and slapping himself all over his pants and shirt. Then he fell onto the ground and started wiggling all over the place and screaming like he was being killed or something.

Wayne and I just thought he was playing a joke on us so he would not have to rake the yard—you know how eight- or nine-year-old boys are. So we just walked back over and picked up our rakes and just stood there looking at him, but he never stopped yelling and screaming or wiggling all over the place. Wayne walked over to Dean and noticed that there were yellow jackets flying out of his shirt and pants. There were hundreds of them everywhere just stinging him over and over and over. He just kept wiggling and yelling and wiggling and yelling for someone to help him.

Wayne hollered at me to go and get the house parents and I ran toward the boys' building. Wayne ran to get the water hose to see if he could spray water on him to get the yellow jackets away from Dean.

I ran into the boys' building and went from room to room looking for the house parents. I found them in the small kitchen downstairs, baking an angel food cake. I told them what had happened to Dean and that he needed help right away, but they said they could not come out until the cake had been taken out of the oven, so I just waited with them until the cake came out so that I could show them where Dean was. I guess it took five minutes or so for them to get the cake out of the oven, and they were complaining the whole time about us kids and what a bunch of idiots we were and that if our parents would have been smart at all they would have taken us out and cut our heads off when we were first born and that the world would be a lot better off. They talked like that all the time and we were used to it. I don't think they really meant any of that stuff anyway, but it sure made you feel real bad sometimes when they talked like that.

Finally, they came to help Dean. He looked real bad. He was covered with stings all over his face, arms, hands, neck, and even in his red hair. He was getting sick and throwing up on the ground. I just kicked some dirt over it and thought I might come back later and pick it up in a shoebox and dump it in the house parents' bed, if I could get up enough nerve or get someone to help me do it.

I figured they had taken Dean to the hospital because I did not see him again for several days. We had heard he was going to die from all the stings he got, so we never went back into the azalea bushes again. We just threw the leaves and pine straw into the bamboo area where no one could see it.

When Dean did come back from the infirmary, which is where they took him, he was a mess. He was all swollen up and had sores all over his freckles. I remember telling him that he looked like a freak, and then he beat me up something terrible.

But we still stayed friends. ❖

THIS WAS MY LUCKY DAY AT THE ORPHANAGE, OR SO I thought, because at breakfast time I got to eat eleven pieces of toast all by myself and I was full for the first time in a long time. Although generally the food at the orphanage was nothing to speak of, I liked the toast that they made in the big metal oven.

The next morning I got in line with the rest of the boys and we marched to the dining room for breakfast. Mrs. Dalbert, the head matron, pointed at me and told me to "get your little seven-year-old bastard ass" back to the boys' building. She said that I was not going to get any breakfast at all that morning because I did not drink my powdered milk the day before. So I walked back to the dormitory by myself and went upstairs and sat in my room looking out the window at the dining-room building where all the other kids were eating.

Later that day, I was called to the office and told to report to the nursery to see some new people. When I arrived, there was a man sitting in a chair in one of the side rooms and he was holding a great big red apple in his hand. He told me to sit down in the other chair and he began to talk to me about why I looked so sad. I told him that I was sad that day because I was very hungry. "Would you like this big red apple?" he asked me. "It sure would taste good," I told him. "If I give you this apple, then you will have to do something special for me," he said, with a big smile on his face. "Okay," I told him, shaking my head up and down real hard.

The man got up off his chair and walked over to the door and closed it. Then he walked back over to where I was sitting and stood before me. He reached down and started unbuttoning his pants and then he took out "his thing." "Can you touch this for me?" he said. "I can't do that. That would be a bad thing," I said. "Do you want this big red apple?" he asked. "Yes sir," I said. "Then you have to touch it for me," he told me. "I can't touch that 'cause that's a wrong thing to do," I said, looking away from him.

He raised me by the arms and up from my chair, then laid me down on the hard tile floor. Then he laid on top of me, with all my clothes on, and began to make all kinds of different sounds and noises. One time he even pulled my hair and squeezed my face and it hurt real bad too, and I told him "don't do that no more." Then he got up and fixed his pants and told me to get back into my chair. He took a great big bite out of the side of the big red apple and then he handed it to me, telling me that I could now have it and that I could leave and go back to the boy's building, where I lived with my friends.

When I got back to the dormitory, I told all the other boys that he was a really bad man and that he gave me a disease. Later that evening, Mrs. Dalbert called me to her office and asked me why I was telling all the other kids that the old man had given me a disease. I told her that the man was bad because he had promised to give me the big red apple but then he took a great big bite out of the side before giving it to me. My schoolteacher had told us that eating after other people would give you a bad disease.

She asked me what I had done with the apple and I told her that I had thrown it over the chain link fence and that it had rolled way out into the schoolyard, next door to the orphanage. I told her that I was really hungry and that I had really wanted the apple. Mrs. Dalbert took me into the big kitchen pantry and gave me some dried prunes and apricots and then she told me that I had best forget about the man who came to see me and that I was not to say anything more to anyone, ever! ❖

THE SCHOOL BELL RANG, AND EVERYONE WAS GOING inside. Nathan Lawrence and I were in the third grade and had decided to skip school and go over to this man's yard and eat some of his fruit. There were big trees in his yard with lots of oranges, pears, and grapefruit. We had never had pears or oranges before, but we knew they must be worth risking trouble for. We traveled down a long fence and went into his back yard and hid in the bushes. We sat there for about an hour, just watching to make sure that no one was home. Then, we went into his yard and started eating the pears and oranges. Delicious.

As we ate, we noticed there was something moving in the pond. We walked over to the pond and noticed that there were large fish swimming around in it. We had never seen anything like them before. These fish were a golden color. They weren't big enough to eat—but they were big enough to catch. However, they were too fast for us, and the pond was too deep to get in. We looked around the yard and found an old cane fishing pole. We went into the flower bed and dug up several worms and placed one on the hook. Within several seconds we had caught our first fish, the first fish we had ever seen up close. It was alive and shaking all over the place, so we put it back into the water.

The next thing we knew, this man came walking out the back door. He was walking really slow toward us. He just looked at us and said, "Do you boys like to fish?" We told him that we were sure we would but that we'd never been fishing before because we were from the orphanage. He told us that the fish we were catching were not for fishing, that they were for decoration. He called them "goldfish" and said that they could not be eaten. Then he took us into his house and gave us something to drink. Next, he got a large paper bag and took us back out into the yard. He told us to help him fill the bag with oranges and pears. After the bag was full, he handed it to us and told us that we could take it back to the orphanage with us. He put us in his car and took us back to The Children's Association.

Needless to say, we did not get any of those oranges or pears. I remember the man telling Nathan and me that he would come back one day and take us fishing. But he never came back. And Nathan and I got a beating and were sent to our rooms without any supper.

The next day I went into the downstairs bathroom and was sitting on the toilet. After I finished using the toilet, I reached up and grabbed the toilet paper. As I unwound the paper, something bit me on the finger. When I looked down, I saw a scorpion lying on the floor. I jumped off the toilet, pulled my pants up, and then stomped on the scorpion until it was dead and flat. Then I picked it up very slowly with some toilet paper and ran to get the house parent. I was yelling and crying because I was really scared. I had heard that scorpions were poisonous and that people died from scorpion bites.

I found the house parent sitting on the front porch. I told him what had happened, and I showed him the scorpion. I asked him to help me, please, for I was going to die if he did not get me to a doctor. He told me to get my little ass up to my bedroom. Furthermore, he said that if I died, it was punishment for having fished in that guy's fish pond and having stolen his fruit. I will never forgive that house parent for making me wait in my room to die, far worse than getting no supper. ❖

I RAN AS FAST AS I COULD, CRYING ALL THE WAY, OVER TO THE high chain link fence that surrounded the orphanage. I pressed my teary-eyed face against the cold rusty holes and with all my might I pushed the heavy steel wire outward with my hands. I looked, as best I could, to the right and then to the left to see if "Old Topper," the policeman who walked around the orphanage fences every afternoon to check on things in the neighborhood, might be walking by. But he was nowhere in sight.

As I turned around and placed my back against the fence, still shaking and crying from fear, I saw the matron beating one of the boys on the back of his head with the broken, old, rusty pogo stick that we had found laying on the edge of the baseball diamond at the Spring Park Elementary School. Many of the boys heard the loud screams that were coming from the nursery playground, as well as the matron yelling at the top of her voice at the young boy. They all started gathering around to find out what was happening. No one said anything, however, because we knew better to keep quiet or risk being the next in line.

I stood against the fence, shaking for fear that the matron would soon look up and see me. If she knew that I too had been trying to jump on the rusty old pogo stick, and that I was trying to tell "Old Topper" what was happening to us kids at the orphanage, she'd beat me for sure. I carefully lowered myself to the ground and slid slowly like a snake on my stomach until I reached the safety of the azalea bushes. My heart was beating ninety miles an hour in my chest and the sides of my head, by my temples, were moving in and out, from the pressure.

I just laid there, real quiet, for the longest time, waiting for the matron to leave. The beaten boy laid there on the ground, at her feet, without moving. Finally, she stopped yelling at him, threw the old pogo stick over the red brick fence, and then walked inside.

I saw the row of boys that was looking out the window start to disappear one at a time for fear that the matron might catch them. Looking out the windows was something that was absolutely forbidden for us to do under any circumstances.

After about five minutes, I slowly snuck out of the thick green azalea bushes and made my way over to the edge of the red brick nursery building so that I could whisper to the little boy who was laying on the ground, still not moving.

"Hey," I whispered to him. "Hey, you ok?" I said to him a little louder. But there was no answer. I carefully walked over to the little boy and when I did, I saw that his eyes were open real wide and that they were rolled back into his head like some sort of monster creature. I put my hand on his face very gently because I didn't want to touch him if he was dead.

As I felt him on the face with my finger, he moved just a little bit and then he turned his face over and looked at me.

There was some blood coming out of his ear, but I didn't say anything to let on that he was near death. "Will you play the pogo with me?" he said. I did not know what to say back to him so I just sat down beside him and put my hand on his head.

"What is going on?" yelled someone off in the distance. My heart started beating fast again and I jumped up quickly and started to run back to the azalea bushes, but my arms started shaking badly and I could not stop them so I started crying and screaming. The next thing I knew I was laying on the ground and I was looking up at Old Topper. "Are you alright, son?" he asked. "It's the little boy over there," I said, as I pointed in the boy's direction. "He's gonna die real soon 'cause he got blood comin' out of his ears."

When I finally sat upright, I saw the matron running out of the nursery toward us. I looked up at Old Topper and I begged him to help us get out of the orphanage. But he just told me that it was my home now and that we should be thankful to have such a good place to live and food to eat.

The matron, Mrs. Towers, took Old Topper over to where the little boy was now standing and I heard her tell him that he had fallen off the pogo stick and hit his head on the concrete. She rubbed the little boy on the hair and hugged him the whole time that Old Topper was there. She just kept looking at me real mean like so I just kept nodding my head as though I was saying "yes" the whole entire time.

I never did tell Old Topper what really happened to the little boy and he didn't die like I thought he would. But I did ask Old Topper for a stamp, which he gave to me, so that I could write a letter and mail it to someone important.

That night I made my own envelope out of a piece of white notebook paper that I stole out of an older boy's locker and I went in the bathroom, after the matron was asleep, and I wrote a letter to President Eisenhower, leader of the United States of America, and I told him what had happened to that little boy. But I never heard back, ever. I guess he thought that I was lucky too, just like Old Topper did. ❖

I WAS PLAYING IN THE YARD WHEN I WAS CALLED TO THE matron's room. She told me to report to the nursery across the "circle," a grassy area in the center of the orphanage grounds. I immediately walked over to the nursery and was told to go into one of the playrooms on the left side of the hallway. I did as instructed.

Several minutes later this dark-haired woman came in and told me that she wanted to talk with me, that she wanted to give me some tests. I sat down on a small chair and then she sat down in front of me, about ten feet or so away. She asked me to tell her my name and how old I was. I believe I told her I was seven.

She asked me a little about this and that. Then she started to say things that she thought would make me laugh. I guess she was trying to make me feel comfortable. Then she got up and walked behind me and started rubbing my shoulders and neck. Right out of the blue she said, "Do you know the difference between a boy and a girl?"

I did not say a word. I just sat there. She then walked around in front of me and stood there for a minute or so. Just looking and staring at me with a smile on her face. Then she told me to stand up and take my shirt off.

I slowly got up and began to remove my shirt. She took the shirt and wiped it across my face and then laughed. "Isn't that better?" she said.

Still, I just stood there real quiet and scared. Then she went back to her chair and sat down. Again, I just stood there, too scared to do or say anything. She bent forward in her chair and looked at me and said, "What is the difference between a girl and a boy?"

"I don't know," I said.

"Are you sure you don't know?" she said.

I just stood there, shaking my head, no.

She got off her chair and walked toward me. She stopped about two feet in front of me and said, "I want you to take off your pants."

I just stood there, like a dummy. I did not know what to do. I started crying as the woman started to unbuckle my belt. I quickly sat down in my chair and started crying even harder.

She bent down and said that everything was going to be all right. She raised me up by the arms and stood me on my feet. She pulled my belt off and stood there looking at me. She slowly raised the belt into the air and said, "I will ask you again. What is the difference between a girl and a boy?"

"I DON'T KNOW!" I yelled at her.

She grabbed me by the arm and shook me real hard and said, "You take those damn pants off young man. Do you understand me?"

"Yes, ma'am," I said.

I stood up and started to unbutton my pants, but I could not get the button to come loose because I was shaking so badly. Then she grabbed me and pushed me backward into the chair. "Stand up!" she yelled.

I once again stood up and started to cry so hard that I was shifting backward and forward and gasping for air.

"I know you know the difference between a girl and a boy!" she screamed.

She then took her finger and started poking me on the end of the nose. "If you do not tell me the difference between a girl and a boy right now, young man, I am going to make you take your pee-pee out in the dining room and show it to everyone. Do you understand that?"

I looked at her and she waved the belt at me. I started unbuttoning my pants and let them drop to the floor. She reached over and slid my underpants down around my ankles. She grabbed my penis and pulled it out straight so that it stretched outwards.

"What is this?" she said.

"I don't know, ma'am," I said.

Then she pulled on my penis real hard and it hurt real bad.

I started to run for the door, but I tripped because my pants and underwear were down around my ankles. I reached down and halfway pulled up my pants and underwear, then I started running for the doorway.

"You be in that dining room tonight, do you hear me?" she yelled.

I ran as fast as I could and hid in the bushes near the boys' building.

I stayed in the bushes for two days without coming out. I slept under the Spring Park Elementary School at night, because the sand was warm under there. I only came out because Joe Wilson found where I was hiding. He told the office where I was. I think he got a watermelon for turning me in.

I never liked the word "pee-pee" after that. Watermelon either. ❖

I T WAS MAY DAY AND ALL THE CHILDREN FROM THE SPRING Park Elementary School had gathered on the school grounds for the May Day Maypole dance. This dance involves many short flagpoles with six streamers attached to each pole. As the music plays, the six children holding the streamers weave in and out of one another until the streamers are tightly woven around the Maypole. Then everyone claps and yells and the celebration begins. There are lots of races and games, food concessions, and the like.

On this particular day, the weather was quite cold, and it looked as if there might be rain. Several of the boys from the orphanage walked around the school grounds, just looking at who was doing what. We each had several nickels, so we decided to go buy donuts from one of the concession stands. As we got there, it started raining really hard. Everyone started running for the school building. It was sheer madness around there, so much madness that I decided to reach over and get myself a free donut. I had never had a donut before. Besides, they were going to get all wet and be ruined. And since they were all going to be ruined, I ate two or three more, just to keep them dry, of course.

It rained and it rained and it rained. Finally I grabbed several boxes of donuts and went underneath the donut table to try to stay dry, though I was already soaked to the bone. I just sat there under that table and kept eating as many donuts as I could eat before the rain stopped. After about twenty or thirty donuts, I did not feel so good. Besides my hand was sore where I had bitten it several times from trying to eat the donuts so fast.

The rain just got harder and harder. Water was coming under the table where I was sitting, so I got up onto my knees. About that time I heard these two boys run up to the table, talking about grabbing the cash box that had been left on the table. When they grabbed the cash box and tried to run with it, they dropped it on the ground. All I saw was what seemed like millions of dollars and coins going everywhere. The boys grabbed as much as they could and started running across the school grounds. I never saw their faces, and I did not know who they were, but I knew they were not from the orphanage because I would have known their voices.

As I sat there, I began to pick up the coins that were left on the ground. I started putting them in my pocket, and soon my pockets were full of money. Then a lady came running out of the school and started yelling at everyone to go home, that the celebration had been called off because of the weather. When she left, I crawled out from under the table and headed back to the orphanage because it was still raining like heck. When I returned, I went to my room where I opened up my closet door and neatly stacked all the coins into rows according to their size.

I was a rich son-of-a-gun, and I knew it. Those Brinks guys think they feel good? They don't know nothin'.

Not being too smart, I decided to show several of the boys what I had in my closet.

BIG MISTAKE.

The next thing I knew, the house parent had me by the collar of my shirt and was dragging me down the front stairs. I broke loose and ran back up the stairs. I was going to run down the upstairs hallway and down the back stairs in order to lose him and avoid the beating I knew he intended to deliver. As I reached the landing in the center of the back stairs, something hit me in the head. My head hit the wall, almost knocking me out. When I looked up, I saw the wooden stool he had thrown at me rolling down the stairs. I just kept running as fast as I could, running to where I don't know—just running.

Needless to say, I was the loser in that ordeal. I was accused of stealing all the money and had to work cleaning up the school grounds for several months. The raking and picking up of leaves stopped only because they beat me until I finally admitted that I had hidden the dollar bills in the ground somewhere.

Of course, the beatings continued anyway because I could not remember where I had buried the money. I dug hole after hole and was beaten with a switch for weeks, trying to find money that I had not taken in the first place.

When you are an orphan, it doesn't do any good to tell a lie. Doesn't do any good to tell the truth, either. ❖

THIS WAS GOING TO BE A VERY EXCITING NIGHT AT THE Children's Association. I could hardly wait for our bedtime so that we could pull off the trick that we had heard about from one of the boys in our second grade class. He told us that you could take a bowl of warm water, and when someone fell asleep, you could stick his hand into the warm water and he would wet on himself. We wanted to test this out on one of the boys who was somewhat of a bully to the rest of us.

As night fell and the house parents settled down for the night, we went into the large bathroom and, with our hands cupped under the sink spigot, we prepared our solution of warm water in an old metal wash bucket used for scrubbing the hallway floors, and headed down the long, dark hallway to the bully's bedroom.

There he was, right in front of us, dead asleep, with his fat face stuffed into the pillow. He was making all kinds of snoring and smacking sounds with his mouth. Everyone kept looking at each other to see who had guts enough to pick up the metal bucket and stick his hand into the warm water. While scheming, we'd never discussed who was going to do what, so we just stood there making excuses with one another.

All of a sudden the hall light came on and there stood the house parents. "Just what the hell is going on here?" said the woman. "We were just getting a drink," said one of the boys. "Come here, right now!" the man hollered at us. We all slowly walked toward him and finally stopped where the hallway turned to the left to go down the front stairway. "What's in the damn bucket?" said the man. "Just water," I said to them. "Water for what?" asked the man, as he reached out and grabbed one of the boys by the hair. "It's pee water. It's pee water," yelled the little boy. "It's not really pee water," I told the matron, hoping that she would believe me.

The man reached over and picked up the bucket and looked inside and said, "It looks like pee water to me. What were you boys going to do—pour this on someone's bed and get them in trouble?" "No sir," I said. "It's not really pee water, sir. It was just a trick that we were going to play for fun." "Damn tricks are not for kids. Do you little bastards understand that?" he said.

"Get in a straight line," yelled the man. I thought for sure he was going to march us down to the sewing room for a beating, but we were lucky that night to escape without one. All we had to do that night was to get in a straight line and take turns drinking all the "pee water" that he thought was in the bucket. We sure acted like it tasted horrible too! ❖

ONE DAY I WAS CALLED OVER TO THE NURSERY TO SEE Mrs. Towers because I was accused of shaking the chain-link fence at some of the children who were playing on the baseball field outside of the orphanage fence. The non-orphan children would almost always make fun of us kids who were locked away in the orphanage.

When I arrived at the nursery, Mrs. Towers wanted to know why I was shaking the fence at the children on the ball field and I told her that they were making fun of us again. She told me that she was going to whip me and that I had better not ever shake the fence again. When she walked out of the room, I ran out behind her and started running down the hallway. She got a large paddle and started chasing me but could not catch me.

Finally, I lost her somewhere outside of the building and I ran back inside and into her bedroom and got underneath her bed. I lay there for a while and then noticed that there was a large box at the head of her bed. I opened the box and found hundreds of letters that were addressed to the children at the orphanage.

I did not think anything of it until I came across a red envelope that had "Master Roger Dean Kaiser" written on it. My name was Roger Dean Kaiser (spelled Kaiser at the time), but who the hell was "Master"? I opened the envelope and read the card inside and it was signed, "your grandpa, Michael Parker," and it was from Alaska, wherever that was.

There were other letters there too, for Dean Whitcomb, Russell Wagner, Wayne Evers, and Eddie Gillman, but I did not think anything about it. Then Mrs. Towers came into her room and made me climb out from under her bed. She looked under the bed and saw all these letters and cards all over the floor and she got real mad at me. Then she spanked me and made me eat two whole letters and the red card from Michael Parker.

It took me a long time to eat all that paper because it was hard to swallow, but I got it down. She told me that if I ever told anybody that she would report me to the post office people and they would take me to jail for messing with other people's mail. So I never told anybody until now.

After that I could not use the bathroom for two or three days, and I was hurting really bad in my stomach. I tried and tried to go to the bathroom, but nothing would come out of me. Eventually, I was hurting so bad that I got a toothbrush handle and started digging the hard stuff out of me that way. I will not go into any more detail than that. But I want to make this point: that is the way it is when you are raised in an orphanage. There is nowhere for a child to turn even for the most private, personal things.

Years later, in 1963, I found Mr. Michael Parker in Anchorage, Alaska, when he was on his deathbed. It was the first and last time I ever saw him. He held my hand and told me that he loved me and he wanted to know why I never wrote him back. But how could I tell this dying man that someone made me eat his letters without reading them, that I never knew who he was when it would have mattered the most. ❖

ONE OF MY TEACHERS AT SPRING PARK ELEMENTARY School was Mrs. Horner. She was a good teacher, but she was very strict with her students. Students were there to learn, and she was going to teach them, like it or not.

I had a very difficult time learning, especially English and math. But there was one thing I was good at: I was very fast at counting on my fingers. So one day Mrs. Horner called me to the front of the class and made me stand by the blackboard. One at a time she called the other children up to the blackboard and called out a math problem that they wrote on the blackboard. Then Mrs. Horner would say, "Go," and we would find the answer to the problem. What Mrs. Horner was trying to show me was that adding or subtracting in one's head was much faster than counting on fingers.

"Wrong, Mrs. Horner," I thought to myself.

There must have been twenty-five children in our classroom. I had the answer before about fifteen or twenty of the children, before some smart-aleck girl tied with me. Then Mrs. Horner made me hold one of my hands behind my back and race the same girl again. The entire classroom was yelling and screaming with laughter. I was also laughing. When Mrs. Horner said, "Go," I yelled out the answer before the girl had a chance to figure out the first set of numbers. This really made Mrs. Horner mad, especially now that the class was laughing so loud that Mrs. Drayer, the principal, came in from the office to see what was happening. Mrs. Drayer was also laughing and said that she was amazed that a child could count so fast by hitting his fingers against his leg.

Mrs. Drayer made me feel very proud that I could do something that no one else could do. No one in the whole wide world could do what I was doing. There was no one faster at counting on his or her fingers than I. No one. Finally, I had found something that this orphan boy could do that no other "normal" kid could do. The orphan finger was faster than a normal kid's brain!

Well, I couldn't beat anyone at counting when my two pointy fingers were stuck in my "big ears" for the next two school days.

Thanks a lot, Mrs. Horner. ❖

I THOUGHT IT MUST HAVE BEEN A MIRACLE, BECAUSE WE orphans were going to get to watch a television show called *Corky and White Shadow*. It was about a kid and a big white dog and we were very excited about being able to see it. Watching television was not a common occurrence at the orphanage, because most often we were cleaning to make things look nice and new.

The television was turned on and all us boys sat up real straight and proper so that we would not get sent to our rooms and miss this wonderful opportunity. I remember moving my eyes around very slowly, without moving my head, and seeing all the smiles on the boys' faces, and I remember the matron walking around the room in a great big circle, just looking for someone to slouch so he could be sent to his room and miss the show.

But everyone was minding their manners and the matron was becoming very upset and kept hitting the back of a chair with her paddle. Some of the boys started laughing and then tried to cover their mouths so that the matron would not hear them. She must have heard something, though, because one of the boys got hit on the side of the face with the wooden paddle anyway, and it knocked his glasses off his head, shattering as they hit the metal radiator.

I didn't dare say a word. One of the boys called her a "fatty" in a soft voice, and she then started wildly swinging the paddle at everyone. One by one, we all started scurrying to try to get out of her reach. In the end, she made us walk past her, as she stood in the doorway and took a swipe at each of us as we passed by. We were all sent to our rooms.

It was still daylight, so when I got to my bedroom, I went over and looked out of the upstairs window and saw an old station wagon driving up to the office of the head matron, Mrs. Dalbert. Two grownups got out of the old car, with two small children in tow. I watched them walk around the car for several minutes, staring at them and trying to imagine what it must be like to live in a normal house with parents, to be able to watch shows like *Corky and White Shadow,* and to have a big white dog of my own.

The next thing I remember, I heard a scream from the bedroom next to mine, coming from one of the kids who was new to the orphanage. "It's my mommy, it's my mommy!" he kept crying out at the top of his voice. The matron came running down the hallway as fast as she could, and she ran into his bedroom and started beating on him with a belt. We all went to our doorways and slowly peeked our heads out, but we could not see anything. We could hear that she was beating on that little kid, who was all of three or four years old, real hard. He was placed on our wing of the orphanage only temporarily, as he was waiting to go live in the nursery building, which was located across the orphanage grounds on the other side of the big grass circle.

I ran back to my bedroom window again, but all I could see was the old station wagon driving out the back gate of the orphanage. The two little kids were now standing by Mrs. Dalbert, over by the dining room office building, and they were both crying something fierce. The next day I learned that these two children were the brother and sister of the young boy who was being beaten in the bedroom next to mine.

The next day I put my arm around the little boy when we were sitting out on the dining room porch waiting to eat supper, and I told both the new kids that everything would be okay and that one day soon they would forget how to cry, just like all the rest of us. ❖

ONE MORNING I WAS LINED UP AT THE LAUNDRY ROOM door to get my clothes for the day. This particular morning I really wanted to look special because a new girl had just come to our second grade class and she was assigned to sit right next to me, and she kept looking and smiling at me a whole lot. I think she liked me because the other kids were making fun of me for counting on my fingers instead of counting with my brain like the teacher said to do.

When I got into the line with the other boys to get my clothes that day, I saw a pretty green-and-white-striped shirt down near the bottom of the big pile of clothes. So I kept moving backward in the line so that I could get in just the right spot to get the green-and-white shirt when the matron finally got down to it. It worked, too, because I made it just at the right time and she handed me the shirt and a pair of light brown short pants, and then she laughed and called me "Mr. Khaki Short Pants." I was so very happy that day that I ran all the way upstairs and began to put my good clothes on, smiling real big and yelling as loud as I could with excitement. I was really glad because I was going to be happy that day when the new girl saw me in my nice green-and-white shirt and khaki pants.

When I went to put on the shirt, I noticed that the collar had been cut off and I almost cried because "I don't like looking like I didn't have no collar," I told one of the boys. But one of the older boys told me they had seen one just like it before and that it was made that way in the factory and that the rich people who bought nice clothes probably wore that shirt and then gave it to us by accident. Now I was really happy, all over again, because I was getting to wear a rich person's shirt. I couldn't wait to go back to school to see that girl in my class and learn how to count numbers with my brain.

After we were all dressed for school, all the orphans once again lined up and the orphanage people handed us one nickel each to buy our milk at school, and then they handed us our brown paper bag lunch. I started walking toward the school, which was right next to the orphanage outside the large fences and white gates. When no one was looking, I ducked into the azalea bushes and buried my brown paper bag lunch underneath a pile of leaves so the new girl in my class would not see it and know that I was from the orphanage. Everyone from everywhere knew that only the orphans carried a brown paper bag lunch to school every day.

I brushed off the leaves from my knees and then I came back out of the bushes and headed toward the school. When I turned the curve and walked outside of the large white orphanage gates, several of the boys who were always making fun of us ran up behind me and tore the back pocket off my brown pants and then threw it over the fence and ran away, laughing as hard as they could. I tried to look at the back of my pants, but I couldn't see that far behind me. So I took out my shirttail and tried to cover the tear in my pants, but it wouldn't cover it up very well.

I decided I would not go to school that day because of my torn pants and that I would just take the beating when the orphanage found out that I had skipped school. That way the girl in my class would think that I was just sick that day and couldn't come to school, and then everything would be okay and she could start liking me all over again the next day.

I walked very slowly past the school and down to some houses so I could find a place to hide all day until I saw all the other kids going back to the orphanage when school got out. But then I decided to run back to the orphanage and grab the lunch that I had buried in the leaves so I wouldn't be so hungry all day long. Then I ran back out the gate to look for a place to hide until the school let out that afternoon.

In a little while I saw two police cars going through the orphanage gate and then I knew that the school had called the head matron and that she had telephoned the police. Now they were going to get me and put me in those big chains like Eddie Gillman and take me to the big prison. That is what Mrs. Dalbert said they would do to me if I was ever bad again, or ever ran away again. It was too late for me to be good now. I tried to think of a way that I could go back and not get my pants torn by those boys. Then I could just go on to school like before, like nothing had ever happened at all. But I couldn't make what happened become undone, so I could not start all over again. It was too late now, and I was really scared.

I started walking really fast back to the orphanage, and when I entered the large white gates I walked directly toward the police cars sitting near Mrs. Dalbert's office. One of the policemen saw me first and then Mrs. Dalbert pointed at me and they all started running toward me. I was really scared and started running toward the girls' dormitory, with them chasing me. I ran as fast as I could and jumped up onto the large wire fence to get away because the gates were just too far away. I tried to climb over the high fence, but the policeman grabbed me by the shirt and jerked me off the fence and into the dirt pile, and then he jumped on top of me and held me down until Mrs. Dalbert got there.

Mrs. Dalbert grabbed me by the shirt and pulled me up off the ground and called me a "big-eared little #@#&$." I don't remember much after that because my brain wouldn't work—I was just too scared to think anymore. I do remember asking Mrs. Dalbert to let me keep my shirt, but I never saw it again after that. The other boys told me that it was kept as evidence against me so they could put me in prison one day to get rid of me for good. ❖

EASTER HAS NEVER BEEN A GOOD TIME OF THE YEAR FOR me. The first one I can remember was when I was seven years old, and I still remember it to this day. "Here comes Peter Cottontail, hoppin' down the bunny trail." The words to that song will forever stay with me, and not out of fondness.

It was about six-thirty on Sunday morning when the matron knocked on our bedroom doors and told us to get up and start getting ready for church. I walked into one of the two large bathrooms and began washing my face in the porcelain sink when all of a sudden someone slapped me in the back of the head and told me to hurry along as the other boys were already lining up to march over to the dining room for break-fast before getting on the church bus.

I didn't like going to church very much. You had to sit per-fectly still on that hard church bench, for over an hour, and if you coughed or moved at all, you'd get swatted hard on the leg, creating great big black and blue bruises all over you. I liked being a Methodist and all, whatever that means, but they just hit on us kids too much to be really good people.

But I really did like Sunday school. It was fun and I learned a lot from what Jesus said when he lived here. I could say all the books of the Bible by heart, and in order too, and I could say John 3:16 without taking a breath. I liked holding the Bible 'cause it felt good and I liked the really shiny pictures and especially the red writing that told what all Jesus said.

But after we ate breakfast, I was told that I would not be going to Swain Memorial Methodist Church that Sunday. I was told to go back to the boys' building and change out of my Sunday clothes and then to report to Mrs. Dalbert, the head matron.

After changing my clothes, I walked back to the dining room and sat in the screened-in breezeway and waited for Mrs. Dalbert to come out and tell me what to do. All of a sudden this strange man came walking out of the glass doors, which led from the large dining room. He was carrying lots of colored eggs in big flat boxes and he told me that I was going to get to help him hide the eggs so that all the orphans could hunt for them after they got back from church. I was so excited that happy Easter day because I was the only kid who would know where all the eggs were hidden.

Me and that nice man hid lots and lots of eggs all over the big grass circle out in the center of the orphanage grounds, as well as in the big oak tree where I once got hung by the neck by Mr. Spoon, that time.

After we got done hiding all the eggs, we walked back to the dining room so we could get a drink of cold water. Then we sat down on the steel chairs in the breezeway and we talked about church and about me being a good boy and especially about me minding older people. We talked about church for about ten minutes and then I told him that I could say all the books of the Bible without missing any at all. He had me stand up in front of him and repeat all the books of the Bible and when I got all done he laughed and clapped his hands for me. I was laughing and smiling real big too, 'cause I was real proud of myself. I was the only boy in the orphanage who could say all the books of the Bible and I was going to heaven one day and I could say them for Jesus and then he would hug me just like he did all the little children in the shiny Bible pictures.

The next thing I remember I was in the bathroom, by the hallway closet, with this man and he didn't have any clothes on and he was telling me to undress. He told me that because we hid the eggs and didn't get to go to Easter Sunday church service that we had to get down on our hands and knees and be cleansed by the spirit.

I just cannot tell you the rest of the story because it is just too horrible to see written in bad words. But I will always remember that smiling, ugly, naked man standing up in front of me and singing those words, "Here comes Peter Cottontail, hopping down the bunny trail. Hippety hoppety Easter's on its way." ❖

AT EIGHT YEARS OLD, I DID NOT REMEMBER EVER BEING loved, held, or hugged by anyone, not even one single time. I guess I thought that being loved or cared about really did not matter very much because I did not know that such a feeling even existed.

One day I was playing in the dirt pile out behind the boys' dormitory, when I heard this strange noise coming from behind me. I immediately jumped up and spun around because I thought I was in trouble again, as usual, with the matron. When I stood up I saw the most beautiful, kind, and loving face looking directly at me. The eyes of an angel were looking only at me, and my heart skipped a beat for the first time in my young life. I placed both of my hands over my cheeks, took in a deep breath, and with my eyes and mouth open as wide as saucers, I backed up very slowly against the oak tree and just waited to see what would happen next.

She just stood there like a statue, looking at me, and she did not say anything at all. My eyes rolled and rolled, as I looked her up and down from head to toe. I noticed the beautiful brown and white coat that she was wearing. After a minute or so I reached out and very slowly touched her coat and she opened her mouth, but then closed it again without making any sound. I quickly withdrew my hand because I did not want to get into trouble, and I placed it behind me to show her that I was sorry for touching her and that I would not do it again. Still she did not say anything at all, so I sat back down in the dirt pile and tried not to make eye contact with her again. Finally she came over to where I was sitting and touched me gently on the face. It was very warm and it felt good to be touched by something that did not want to hurt me, for a change. I just kept looking down at the ground because I did not want to look her directly in the eye. You were not allowed to look anyone in the eye at the orphanage because that was a sign of defying authority.

Finally, I could take it no longer and I grabbed her around the neck and I just hugged her as hard as I could until she let me know that she really did like me, by licking me on the face.

That was the first and only dog we ever had at the orphanage, and I have no idea where she came from. Later that day we boys all named her "Honey." She was a big, old, ugly-looking, brown-and-white bird dog. We loved that dog and that dog loved all of us back with no strings attached.

It was too good to last. About two weeks later one of the boys came running to my room, crying his little eyes out, and told me that Honey had been run over by a car outside the orphanage gate. I ran downstairs as fast as I could and locked myself in the telephone room. I stood there against the locked door, breathing in and out as fast as I could, and I would not come out, not even for supper. I stayed in the locked telephone room and cried all night long. The next day I could not even go out the front gate for fear of seeing Honey lying dead in the road, so I climbed over the orphanage fence in order to get to school.

After school, Mrs. Dalbert, the head matron, called me to the office and told me to go with Old Mack, the black groundskeeper, to get a wheelbarrow and pick up Honey from the road. I shall never forget that sight as long as I live because it was worse than horrible. Her insides were all over the place, and I shall never forget the look on Honey's face, as she lay there dead, with her tongue hanging out. I knew that beautiful old dog would never, ever love me again. I just stood there and cried the entire time we were there and I tried not to smell the odor of death. Old Mack, who was a very kind old man, told me not to look at her. All by himself he moved her into the wheelbarrow and picked up all the pieces and then took her someplace to bury her. I don't know where he buried her and I didn't want to know where.

To this day, I'm still not sure why Mrs. Dalbert did such a cruel thing—making me clean up my own dead dog. But, that's not the point. The point is that no one gave a damn how we children felt. There was never anyone to hold us or to tell us that everything was going to be all right. There was never anyone who even cared when our hearts were torn apart. All the house parents saw was a dead dog in the middle of the road, and "a bunch of whining little bastards." Honey was just another thing in the way . . . just like us kids. ❖

THE DAY AFTER OLD MACK AND I HAD CLEANED UP Honey from the road, I was still feeling low and went outside to sit on the back steps by myself. I noticed something moving in the leaf beds beneath some clumps of bamboo that surrounded a maintenance shed on the orphanage grounds. So I got off the cement step and slowly walked over to investigate. I picked up an old, brown, dried piece of bamboo and started poking around in the leaves where the movement had been coming from. All of a sudden this thing came running at me that looked like a big rat with a long, pointed nose and a long, thin tail without any hair on it. It stopped sharply right in front of me and I pointed the long stick of bamboo at its head to keep it away.

The back door of the orphanage opened and one of the house parents started yelling at me and told me to put the bamboo stick down on the ground. He picked up a red brick and threw it at the large rat, hitting it in the head. The thing started bleeding and went running around in a small circle and then fell over onto its side. The man walked over and picked up the bamboo stick and started poking it in the side. The big rat thing moved a little bit and the man stuck the stick through its neck, making it holler loudly.

"Please let it go," I asked him, but he pulled the stick out of its neck and stuck it through its back end. "It ain't hurtin' nobody," I told him. "Please let it make it to the woods." Then he took the bloody stick and poked me in the back, tearing a hole in my shirt as I pulled back. "It's just a possum," he told me. "I know, but it's alive and it's not hurting anyone," I said to him. Once again he poked me with the bamboo stick and then grabbed me by the back of my shirt. "Stick this stick through his head," he told me. "I don't want to kill nothing," I told him, looking away from the bleeding creature.

The man threw the bamboo stick down onto the ground and then reached into his pocket, pulling out a large knife, which he unfolded. "You poke that stick through his neck and kill it or I'll cut his damn head off," the man told me. "I don't want to kill it," I told him again. The man reached down slowly and cut the thing's tail off and it yelled again, really loud. I could feel myself getting sick, but I did not know what to do.

I reached down and picked up the stick and pointed it toward the possum. I touched it on the face and it opened its mouth and snarled at me like it wanted to bite me. I jumped back and the man started laughing. The man grabbed the stick from my hand and hit me across the leg and then pushed me toward the bleeding animal. I screamed as loud as I could as I fell on top of the bloody possum. I jumped back up as fast as I could and I ran against the shed. The man walked over and picked up the possum's tail and told me to come over to him. I slowly walked over to where he was and he held out the big tail and told me to put it in my pocket. I started backing up, but he grabbed me by the arm and turned me around. He held me against his body and forced the large tail into my pocket. I felt the tail in my pocket because it was still warm. Then it moved in my pocket and I started yelling, screaming and running all around, trying to get it out of my pocket and get it away from me.

The man just kept on laughing as loud as he could. "Every one of you little bastards are nothing but a bunch of damn pussies," he said as he continued to laugh out loud. Then he took the knife and cut the possum's head off while it was still alive. Then he kicked its head with his foot and it rolled a long, long way down the cement driveway.

The man told me to pick up the body and throw it into the metal garbage can and then he went back into the building. I went into the bamboo pile and got another stick, one that did not have blood on it, and I dug a hole and put the poor possum's body in it. I will never forget the head being separated from its body. Several days later I got a shoebox and I buried the possum and its bloody head underneath the large Christmas tree that was in the center of the grass circle in the middle of the orphanage grounds. ❖

"IT'S HOWDY DOODY TIME. IT'S HOWDY DOODY TIME," blared the little black-and-white television we had at the orphanage. "Get your big-eared damn ass out of here and back upstairs," yelled the large matron lady, trying to slap me with her big hand, as I ran past her and out of the television room door like a flash.

As a young boy, I wish there could have been just one Saturday morning in my life when I could have watched *The Howdy Doody Show* without being afraid of getting into trouble, without having to rake leaves and pine straw, clean toilets, or wax checkerboard floors all morning.

I loved Buffalo Bob, Howdy Doody, Mr. Buster, and that princess lady. She was so pretty and seemed so nice, and I had decided that this was going to be the Saturday that I was going to see that show, all the way through, for the first time.

Down the long upstairs hallway I traveled, and down the back staircase I went, as fast as I could. Then I moved very slowly from dark area to dark area, making my way around to the telephone room, and I slowly opened the heavy door leading out into the orphanage yard. I ran around the building as fast as

I could until I could see the open windows of the television room. I sneaked very slowly up to the open window and raised my head so that I could see the small television set, and there he was, Howdy Doody, with all his freckles and moving his head back and forth like he was always happy and glad. That is the part of Howdy Doody that I liked the best: seeing his head bounce around like everything was happy.

The fat matron was laughing at Howdy Doody, but then she stood up when the commercial came on, so I ducked my head down and waited until everything became quiet again. Then I slowly raised my head to see where she was.

BAM went my head as it slammed into the white brick wall. BAM, BAM, and BAM it slammed three more times. "Get your damn ass upstairs and clean those damn bathrooms like you were told," she yelled at me as I fell to the ground. "I will, I will, I will!" I yelled back at her. I started to cry as I ran back around the large two-story white brick building, holding on to my head. "Work is for orphans and niggers," she hollered as I disappeared around the corner.

I made my way up the back staircase and hurried into one of the two large bathrooms and began cleaning the toilets. One of the older boys came in to wash his hands and I told him what the matron had said and I asked him what a "nigger" was. He thought for a moment, looked at me, and said, "I don't know, never heard of that before."

All I knew for sure was that I was a white orphan boy and the word "nigger" had something to do with my situation, so I chose never to use that word in my whole life. ❖

"SHHH," SAID THE SMALL FOUR-YEAR-OLD BOY, HOLDING HIS finger to his lips after I accidentally walked in on him in his bedroom. "It's a secret," he told me very softly, reaching out with both hands to close the wooden door behind me. "What's a . . . ," I started. "Shhh," he said again, shaking his little finger at me. He ran over to his bed, climbed on top, and then looked out of the large glass window and down across the black shingled roof to see if the matron was anywhere to be seen. "Look down the hallway and see if anyone is coming," he whispered at me. I slowly opened the door, stuck out my head, but I did not see anyone coming from either direction.

"What's going on?" I asked him. He waved his hand for me to follow him and we slowly walked down the dark hallway and into one of the two large bathrooms that were located upstairs at the orphanage. He quietly closed the door and instructed me to stand with my back against the door so that no one else could enter. Then he walked slowly backward, intently watching me and the door, until he reached the last toilet stall. Then he got down on his hands and knees and reached as far as he could behind the toilet and pulled out a brown paper bag.

"What is that?" I asked him. "I can't show you yet," he said. "Why?" I mumbled through my gritted teeth to try and scare him into showing me what was in the bag. "It belonged to some rich people with a new car and I'll get into trouble with Mrs. Dalbert if I get caught with it," he replied. He looked down at the floor and then sat down and began to trace each of the individual white tiles with his index finger. I walked over, bent down, and took the package from his arm and peeked inside the bag. But all I could see was another plastic bag with something inside of it. I couldn't tell what it was because the plastic was so thick and dark colored. "Give it back," he demanded, as he snatched it from my hands.

Within the hour we had rounded up four or five of the other orphan boys whom we could trust, and we all headed out across the vacant field behind the boys' dormitory, heading toward the underground fort that we had dug several weeks earlier. It was located out near the large bamboo bushes, which was one of the best hiding spots when the matron had a switch, polo paddle, or leather strap after us. This was the only safe place we could think of to investigate the contents of the bag.

After posting a lookout, we all snuck one by one into our underground fort using the secret entrance—an old rotten piece of wood covered by dirt and pine straw to make it match the surrounding area. The lookout sat in a thin tree that was hidden from view by the large clumps of bamboo that lined the tall metal fences around the orphanage, keeping us hidden from the rest of the outside world.

We gathered up a few leaves, pine straw, and a couple of twigs in order to make a fire inside the fort. We were eager to inspect the contents of the plastic package without having to open our secret doorway to let in some light. We took half of an old towel and laid it in the center of the dirt floor and then placed the plastic package right in the center, staring at it for several minutes and waiting for someone to make a move.

"Open the plastic bag, stupid," said one of the boys. "Open it," I chimed in, looking at Andrew Blake and pointing at the bag with some fire on the end of a stick. Very slowly Andrew rolled the bag over and over so we could try and find where the woven paper tape started on the package.

"Where did this come from?" said Jim. "He stole it from the rich man's car at the office," said Andrew, pointing at the small boy. "I did not; you're a liar," hollered the little boy, who had hid it behind the toilet in the dormitory. "Both of you just shut up and open the stupid bag," said Jim.

Slowly, one of the boys removed the tape and the plastic package was finally opened and set in the center of the towel. As we stared at the package, all of a sudden it just fell over onto its side and a white powder substance spilled all over the place.

"What the heck is that?" asked one of the boys. "I don't know what it is," said Wayne. "I think it's white poison," said another boy. "Why would that man have poison?" asked Andrew. "To kill rats is what poison is for," I told Wayne. "We ain't got no darn rats," said Wayne. "We got roaches and big ants and we got big possum rats," I said, holding out my hands to show them how big they were.

Within minutes our attention was focused back onto the package and the white powder that had spilled from the plastic pouch. One of the boys took a small stick from the firewood pile and pushed the white powder around on the towel. "It's poison all right," said Andrew. "I think they are going to use it to poison us kids and then they can bury us in the big field at night under the blackberry bushes. I bet that's where all the other kids went that disappeared in the middle of the night and we ain't seen 'em no more either." "I ain't seen no little bones in the field when I was playing out there," I told him. "Ain't gonna find no little kids' bones in the field because they bury 'em deep and way, way down and they rot real fast. That's why no one can ever find them," said Jim, looking at the four-year-old boy. "Will my bones rot fast too?" asked the little boy. "Oh, shut up, you little twirp. You ain't got no good strong bones yet. You're too little to have good bones."

The situation was discussed for almost half an hour and it was decided that we would draw pine straws and that the loser would have to taste the white powder and if he died, we would know that the orphanage was going to poison us kids because we ate too much food and nobody really wanted us anyway. We sent one of the boys outside the fort to get some dried brown bamboo so we could smoke it together and have fun one last time before one of us died. We smoked the dried bamboo just like the rich people who smoked cigars. There was nothing finer to us than sitting in a circle in a deep, wet, cold hole in the ground—our retreat from the world—with a warm fire, just smoking and acting like a bunch of rich fellows.

We finished our bamboo cigars and the straws were finally drawn. I don't remember who lost the drawing, but he was not very happy about having to die for the rest of us and we were not very happy about him having to die for us either. We promised him that we would dig him up and clean his bones every day so that they wouldn't rot real fast.

He took some of the white powder between his fingers and slowly raised it to his lips. I closed my eyes and looked away from his face as I did not want to see him die. "I wish my mommy and daddy would have come back for me before I died," he said in a low tone. "Oh, shut up and eat the poison," said one of the other boys. "You can't tell him to shut up when he's fixin' to die," I said. Jim quickly slapped the young boy's hand away from his mouth and the powder flew everywhere and landed all over everyone in the underground fort. "Now we are all gonna die with poison," yelled one of the boys.

All of a sudden the small fire went out and there was nothing but total darkness and total silence beneath that wet, dark, cold ground. All of a sudden the top of the fort was ripped away as if a tornado had suddenly struck us, and there stood the matron with a large leather belt in her fat hand and two very large men with their hands on their hips, looking at us real mean like.

We yelled and screamed and finally jumped out of that top-less underground fort and scattered in every direction. Some of the boys had even climbed the tallest pine trees and were up fifty or sixty feet above the ground so they would not get hit by the leather belt that the matron was now swinging about wildly.

The very last thing I remember hearing before that limb broke and I fell out of that thirty-foot pine tree was the matron yelling at the top of her voice: "Where in the hell did you damn little bastards get that bag of sugar?"

We had never seen or tasted raw sugar before. That was only for the really rich people and I guess for the head matron, Mrs. Dalbert, who kept it hidden from us and used it only for her morning coffee breaks. ❖

AT SCHOOL ONE DAY, OUR TEACHER ANNOUNCED THAT we were going to a museum. I had never heard of a museum before and had no idea what one was. I was a little nervous about going.

I walked up and asked the teacher if she could tell me what a museum was. She sat down at her desk and explained to me that a museum was a special place where things from the past were kept. She said that the museum we were going to see was even more special because it was a museum designed just for children and that everything inside the building was made for and by children.

We children were loaded onto several school buses and off we went, headed somewhere into the great, big city of Jacksonville, Florida. As we were traveling down all these many roads, turning this way and that way, with all kinds of cars and buses around, I could hardly believe all the stores and large buildings I saw. We left the orphanage so infrequently that the sight of the city was something to behold.

As we traveled, many of the children were talking about a "wishing well" that they had seen at the Children's Museum. I was sitting next to Sue King, a girl in my class, so I asked her what a wishing well was, and she told me that you threw money in this white round wooden thing and then you would make a wish and that the wish would come true. "Anything I want will come true?" I asked her. "Anything," she said back to me. I was really excited and could hardly wait to get to the museum so I could see the wishing well.

When we arrived at the museum, we all lined up, single file, and headed into the white building. I walked along with all the children, looking from right to left and then from left to right to see if I could find the wishing well, but it was nowhere to be seen. "Where is the wishing well?" I kept asking. "SHHH!" the woman in the front of the line kept saying. Finally we were allowed to walk around on our own and told not to touch anything with our hands. "Just look, don't touch," they told us. I didn't know who would want to touch all this ugly stuff anyway. None of it was pretty and the kids who made this stuff were probably old by now.

As I walked back toward the front of the building, I saw most of the kids crowded around the front door. As I walked over I could see that the wishing well was behind the front door, sitting back in the corner. That is why I could not find it right off. I made my way to the wishing well and looked inside and saw that there was lots of money lying in the bottom of the well. Several of the kids were throwing money into the well and then closing their eyes for a minute or so. "Why are you closing your eyes?" I asked this one boy. "If you don't close your eyes, your wish won't come true," he said. I closed my eyes real tight and stood there making my wish. He tapped me on the shoulder and said, "You gotta put money in it first or you don't get a wish." "I don't have any money," I told him. "Then you don't get a wish," he said as he walked away.

I didn't know what I was going to do. We didn't get any money at the orphanage home. There wasn't any money to give us because we were poor. But I knew that I wanted to make my wish and that I had to get some money from somewhere and I had to get it right away. I ran around asking the other kids if I could have money to make a wish. But they had already put all their money into the well and made their wishes. I walked up to the lady who was showing us everything in the museum and I asked her if I could have some money. She stopped, looked down at me, and just said, "SHHH," at me again and then walked away.

I saw Sue King standing by the wishing well, so I ran over and I asked her if she had any money, but she told me that all she had left was her milk money. I asked her if she got to make a wish in the wishing well and she told me that she had. I asked her what she had wished for and she told me, "If you make a wish and you tell anyone what it was, then it won't come true."

I walked around for a long time just looking for any money that might have been dropped on the floor so I could make a wish in the wishing well, but I never found any. Finally, I walked back up front where the wishing well was and saw that there was nobody around it. I walked up and looked inside. "Hello down there," I said into the hollow tube. It was strange hearing my voice sound like that. As I bent over again to say something else into the well, I saw a shiny dime lying on top of all the pennies. I knew that wish would come true because a dime was worth a lot.

I looked around behind me and noticed that no one was in the area. So I slowly reached down into the wishing well and tried to reach that dime. Further and further I tried to stretch, but I just could not reach it.

All of a sudden I went crashing head first into the wishing well! Everyone came running out of all the other rooms. Several of the boys started laughing at me and one of the women who worked at the museum called for a man who helped me get out of the well.

I was taken into the office, where the museum people called the orphanage and asked Mrs. Dalbert if she wanted them to take me to the doctor, as I was bleeding on my face and arm. She told them that I was to stay at the museum and that she would send someone to get me. The rest of the children were then loaded onto the buses and returned to Spring Park Elementary School.

One of the women from the orphanage office came to get me in the old station wagon. She did not say anything to me at all. When we arrived back at the orphanage, Mrs. Dalbert took me into the dining room and made me sit down in a chair. She went into her bedroom at the end of the long hallway, and then came out with a bandage, which she stuck to my forehead. Then she took me into the bathroom and made me look into the mirror. On the bandage was written the word "THIEF" in big, blue letters. She told me that I was to wear it the rest of the school day and that if I took it off that I would get nothing to eat for a week. I was returned to school by the lady from the main office who still did not say a word to me.

When I was in the wishing well I got that dime and I made my wish. I wished that God would fix my ears so that they would not stick out so far, so that all the other kids would stop making fun of me and that I could have a girlfriend to like me one day. Several years later I got my wish and someone took me to the Children's Hospital, where they operated on my ears and made them not stick out so far. However, they pinned one ear back further than the other, and because of that I still never got a girlfriend until I was sixteen or seventeen.

Ever since that time, even on my birthday, I have never made another wish. ❖

WHEN I LIVED IN THE ORPHANAGE, I HATED GOING to school. The kids were very cruel to the children who lived in The Children's Association.

The school baseball diamond at Spring Park Elementary School came right up to the orphanage fence. I would stand for hours with my face pressed against the chain-link fence, just watching the "normal" kids playing baseball and swinging on the swings. It was like a child looking through the window of a donut shop, face pressed against the glass, just watching everyone else eat donuts. I shall never forget the loneliness and how separated I felt from the rest of the world. I will always remember all those kids looking and laughing at us.

One day I decided to run away from the orphanage and not go to school. I ate my brown paper bag lunch before I reached the orphanage gate. After all the other children had gone inside the school, I hid behind a house until the school bell rang. Then I ran as fast as I could down the street and away from the school. I walked about five miles to San Marco Square. I had heard that there were many stores there, stores that had every-thing in the world. I looked at all the big buildings—they were huge. I went inside one store that had fake people standing in the window. They were naked too!

As I rounded a corner in the store, I saw it right in front of me, just like on television. I had never seen such a thing in all my eight years on this earth. But there it was, right in front of me. It was the most beautiful thing I had ever seen. I reached out slowly and touched it with my hand. It was pure silver. I slid my finger over each and every one of the diamonds and rubies.

I walked out of that store with the "Fanner 50" tucked beneath my shirt. About a block or two down the street, I took it out and strapped the leather holster to my side. I felt such pride as I walked up and down the streets of Jacksonville, Florida, diamonds and rubies all gleaming in the sunlight. It felt so good to be noticed; it felt so good to be a "normal" little boy.

Well, all that glory was to be short lived. As I walked back to the orphanage, I realized that I could not return to The Children's Association with such a weapon of high quality. So as I passed the school, I hid the gun and holster in the mailbox. I thought that I would return after dark to collect my treasure. When I did return, it was gone—never to be seen again. My guess is that some "normal" kid found it. ❖

ONE OF THE MOST COMPETITIVE THINGS WE EVER DID at the orphanage was to play marbles in the dirt. Every orphan had his own special bag of marbles and its contents were a sign of who you were in the ranking or pecking order. In order for me to establish myself in this order I knew that I would have to collect any and all of the cat's eye marbles that ever made it onto the orphanage property. This became my sole purpose in life and I would beg, borrow, steal, or cheat if it became necessary to collect these little treasures.

One Saturday morning Wayne Evers, Dean Whitcomb, Russell Wagner, Joe Wilson, and I were out back of the boys' building playing in one of our many championship tournaments. Dean Whitcomb was fighting mad because we were complaining that he had a "steelie" marble (a steel marble) and that we did not want him to use it because it would break our glass marbles when he shot real hard. That Whitcomb boy was a good marble player and a hard shooter, too, not to mention that he could cheat even better than I could. However, if you caught him cheating and called him on it, he would beat the hell out of you.

Just about dinnertime the championship was down to several boys and I was one of the lucky ones. I really did not care if I won or not because my strategy was to wait until the boys shot too hard and they would have to run after their marble, which may have traveled ten or twenty feet away. Then I would start stealing all the cat's eye marbles in the dirt circle, replacing them with other types of marbles and then placing them into my pile. Finally I lost, but I decided to stay and see who the winner was going to be.

About twenty minutes later, Mr. Douglas, one of the house parents, came out to see what we were doing and told us to wash up for lunch. By now there were about twenty boys around the circle waiting to see who would be the weekly marble champion. There was lots of yelling and clapping during the last few minutes of the tournament.

At the end, it came down to two boys and only the best and the prettiest marbles were placed into the dirt circle, including Dean Whitcomb's famous steelie marble. Then, for no reason at all, Mr. Douglas walked into the marble circle and started kicking all the marbles as hard as he could so they went flying everywhere. Dean Whitcomb got so mad at Mr. Douglas that I thought he was going to attack him right there on the spot.

I will never forget Mr. Douglas doing that to us. I guess because I could not understand why, and it just did not make any sense to me, at all. But that is just the way it was for us, and it was that way every day of our lives in that orphanage. Even playing at the game of marbles they would not allow us to feel like we were anybody special or that we could do something special.

We never did find all the marbles, not even Dean Whitcomb's steelie. Because of what Mr. Douglas did, none of us really wanted to become the champion for that week. More importantly, none of us ever became champions, even after we grew up. And now I guess I know why. ❖

SOMEONE WAS NICE ENOUGH TO DONATE SEVERAL OLD girls' bicycles to the orphanage. Since they were not men's bikes, we boys were not very excited because we knew that we would never get to ride them. But after one of the boys got caught stealing and riding a bike from the schoolyard, the orphanage officials decided to allow the boys to ride the girls' bikes on one particular Sunday afternoon.

Our house parents, Mr. and Mrs. Douglas, had several of the boys bring the girls' bikes out onto the rocky roadway in the center of the orphanage. We were told that we could ride around the large grass circle three times each and that would be it. I had never ridden a bicycle so I was rather scared and Mr. Douglas was yelling and screaming at us to hurry up and finish.

When it came my turn, I tried to ride the bicycle but could not steer it in a straight line and was going all over the grass and then back out onto the road. Mrs. Douglas's black-and-white dog Jewel was barking at me and chasing me and making me nervous and scared. Finally, I got up some speed and then the dog came running after me, which caused me to fall onto the rocky road. Now Mrs. Douglas was a kind woman, rather quiet most of the time, but when the bicycle landed on top of Jewel with me on top of it all, she and Mr. Douglas began to yell at me.

I got up from the road and began to run away from the bicycle because the Douglases were running at me. I ran into the boys' building and ran to the bathroom because I was bleeding badly. When I looked at my right hand there was a bone showing through the skin. I was really scared at that point but did not know what to do. I could not go to the Douglases because of what happened to their little dog and they would punish me or worse.

I showed it to one of the other boys and we decided to wash my hand off and go into the library and pile a bunch of books on it to push the skin back together. When that did not work, the boy who was helping me had me lay my hand on the homework table and he hit it really hard with a great big book. Boy, did it hurt, and blood went everywhere, but at least the skin was covering the bone again.

Later, Mrs. Douglas called me out onto the front porch and really let me have it. As I sat there, she was petting and hugging her dog and telling it that everything was going to be all right. I just sat there wishing I was that dog and watching the blood still dripping from my hand.

When Mr. Douglas came up onto the front porch, he saw the blood on the floor and asked me what was wrong. I told him that nothing was wrong, but he wanted to see my hand anyway. Then he took me inside and washed off my hand and told me that it was just cut a little bit, and then he poured methiolate all over my hand, which burned like heck and made me yell really loud. Then he told me to stop acting like a baby and said, "Look, knucklehead, get your little ass up to your room and don't come back out," and I did.

Of course, my small hand eventually healed, but my little heart never did. It still hurts today. ❖

ONE SUMMER DAY, AN ORGANIZATION CAME TO THE orphanage to take us to the beach. It was going to be my first visit to the beach, so I was really excited, as were the rest of the orphan children. Besides, we were going to get to see what was outside the fences of the home, something that the other kids at school talked about all the time and something that we rarely got to see. We were going to this wonderful place, where thousands of people would be all running and playing and laughing—this was going to be the most wonderful day of my life.

That morning, Dean Whitcomb, Steven Thomas, and I had taken an old army blanket and were pulling each other up and down the long hallway that we had just waxed. We would stop at the corner where the hallway turned and hold hands all in a line. Then, Dean would touch the light switch cover screw. When he touched the screw, it would send an electrical charge through our bodies. However, it would shock only the last person in line. That last person was whomever happened to come around the corner at that time. Of course, all hell would break loose if the house parents found out what we were doing, but we didn't care because our spirits were high, we were going to the beach.

We arrived at the beach at about nine o'clock in the morning. We were herded down to the water's edge and given a short talk on water safety. Then we were each assigned a partner and told to stay with that person at all times. As usual, the boys were partnered with the boys and the girls with the girls. But this presented a problem, as Steven Thomas and one of the girls did not have a partner of the same sex. So Mrs. Dalbert decided to allow them to swim alone.

Several hours later, I noticed a commotion at one end of a large cement wall. I ran back up the beach and asked someone what had happened; they told me that some kid had drowned. I began to run up and down the beach, looking for all the kids from the orphanage because I thought it might be Dean Whitcomb or Emmett Gillman who had drowned. (They had kept going out into deep water on an inner tube.) By now there were hundreds of people everywhere, and I could not get any closer to the wall because of all the people around the lifeguards. The people were all pushing and shoving one another, I guess trying to see who had drowned or if it was their own kid. People were going crazy, pushing and shoving and cursing at one another.

As I looked around, I saw one of the women from the orphanage gathering all the children into a large group. I walked over and asked one of the boys if he knew who had drowned. He told me he thought that it was Steven Thomas because Steven had become caught up in a riptide and was pulled out into the deep water. I immediately ran back over to the large group of people who surrounded the child. I pushed my way through all the people—and saw Steven lying on the ground. There was a man sitting on Steven's back, pushing and pulling on his arms. Steven's arms were totally limp, just sort of floppy-like. I knew that he was dead. I just stood there looking at his blue face. In a daze, I ran from the large group of people. In a daze, I just walked around the beach in a circle.

I could not forget what I had seen, especially his open eyes, the floppy arms, and all the sand in his mouth. I don't even remember going back to the orphanage. The next thing I remember, I was sitting on the outside of the dining room of the orphanage and everyone was eating watermelon. I guess that would make it a Sunday, as we always got one sandwich and a slice of watermelon for Sunday supper. I could not eat because of thinking about what had happened to Steven. Everyone was talking about the drowning, and I remember telling Andrew Blake that this would not have happened if Mrs. Dalbert had allowed Steven to have a girl as a swim partner. If she had, Steven would be eating watermelon with the rest of us.

Andrew walked over to the other kids and told them what I had been saying, and one of the girls went to Mrs. Dalbert and told her. Mrs. Dalbert called me over and told me to get back on the bench and to keep my big mouth shut. When I returned to the bench and sat down, one of the girls started making a joke about what had happened to Steven. She ate some of her watermelon and then let part of it fall from her mouth onto the ground. Then the girls asked the boys if we knew what it was. I told them that it was watermelon and watermelon juice. They yelled back at us and said that it was Steven's blood and guts. I immediately jumped up and started throwing watermelon rinds at the girls. They all started running and laughing, and Mrs. Dalbert was also laughing. She motioned for me to come over to her, and when I arrived, she slapped me on the back of the head really hard and told me to go out to the basketball court. I was to place my face against the goal post and stand there until everyone else was done eating.

I will never forget how little a life meant to those girls and to Mrs. Dalbert, just how insignificant an orphan life was to the whole world. What if I had drowned? Would anyone be sad for me? Was there anyone in this world who cared if we orphans lived or died? Or were there just too many orphan bodies for anyone to care about any single boy? Though I was only about nine years old, I learned a lot about life that day—and largely through the sacrifices of Steven Thomas. He was my orphan brother, and I will not forget him. ❖

IN THE CENTER OF THE ORPHANAGE GROUNDS THERE STOOD a very large and beautiful oak tree. It appeared to be about a thousand years old to me. It had large trunks that spread out over fifty feet in every direction. I loved that tree, for it was perfect for climbing. That tree fit me like a glove, and my feet always seemed to find just the right spot to climb higher and higher into its tall limbs. I loved to hide in the top of that large oak. There were thousands upon thousands of leaves, and no one in the world could find me or hurt me as long as I was way up high in its safe, encompassing branches.

I had been told many times by the house parents to stay away from that big tree. I was forbidden to climb in it and was told that if I wanted to climb any trees, I could climb up the pine trees. Since the pine trees were only about fifty feet high and did not have any low branches, I guess they figured I could not climb very high. Besides, when we climbed the pine trees, we got sap all over our clothes, and the sap turned our hands black.

One Sunday the children were eating out back of the dining room on the picnic tables. It was our normal Sunday meal of one sandwich and a large piece of watermelon. As I did not eat watermelon because of what had happened to Steven Thomas, I decided to sneak around the building and climb up the big oak tree. When I got around by the big oak tree, I saw a squirrel flying through the air like a bird. I could not believe that a squirrel was flying like that. It was amazing. I thought I had discovered something that the world had never seen before. I thought a bird and a squirrel must have "done it" and made a new kind of bird-squirrel, and I was going to capture it.

I chased that bird-squirrel all over the place. I threw hundreds of acorns at it, and when I would hit it, the bird-squirrel would fly to another spot. Finally, I hit it and it flew to the ground in the center of the circle. So I chased it until it got tired and could not move. I walked up to the bird-squirrel and looked at it. It had skin under its feet that pulled out like wings. I was going to be rich if I could just catch this furry little critter.

As I slowly reached down to pick it up, the darned thing bit me right through the thumbnail and would not let go. I was running all over the place, shaking my hand up and down as fast as I could, but the bird-squirrel would not let go of me. I was yelling and crying and crying and shaking, but the bird-squirrel would not turn me loose. Finally, I stepped on his tail; he turned me loose and ran up the big oak tree.

I ran back over to the dining room and up to Mrs. Dalbert. I told her that I had been attacked by some creature flying through the air and that it had bitten me, that I was just getting a drink out of the sprinkler when it sneaked up and got me from behind. I just stood there, shaking my hand up and down. Mrs.

Dalbert told me to go and sit down, that she would have Mr. Spoon take a look at my hand in a few minutes.

I went over to the other kids and told them what I had seen. Of course, they did not believe me and started laughing at me. Then Mr. Spoon called me to the side and took a look at my thumb. I told him about the thing I had seen, and he told me that he and I would go back later and capture it.

After dark, Mr. Spoon came to the television room with a rope and told me to go with him so that we could catch the bird-squirrel. We walked out into the center of the grass circle where the big oak tree was located. He told me to climb up the tree and place the rope over one of the branches, that we were going to set a trap for the bird-squirrel. He said that if we caught it, we would both be rich. I climbed up the tree and placed the rope over the branch as he instructed.

After I climbed down from the tree, he asked me to come over to him. He told me to hold on to the rope and to pull on it as hard as I could to make sure that the rope would not break when we caught the creature. I pulled and pulled and pulled on the rope, and it did not break. I asked Mr. Spoon how a little bird-squirrel could break such a big rope. He told me that he was not worried about the creature breaking the rope but that he did not want it to chew through the rope before we could get something to put it in. Then Mr. Spoon told me that we were ready to catch the creature but that there was one more test that we had to make.

He made a large loop on the end of the rope and asked me to put it around my neck, which I did. Then Mr. Spoon pulled on the rope until my feet left the ground. I was choking and kicking; I could not breathe. But he just kept on pulling me higher and higher up into the tree. Finally, he let me down. I fell to the ground and tried to catch my breath. Then he asked me why I had been trying to climb the big oak tree while the other children were eating supper. I told him that I was not in the tree when the creature bit me. Then he pulled on the rope again until I was spinning all around in a circle on my tiptoes. I could not breathe, but he just kept yelling at me to admit that I had climbed up the big oak tree.

After I admitted that I was in the tree, he let me down and told me to go up to my room and go to bed. He said he was going to stay out there and catch the creature; then he was going to bring it to my room and put it into bed with me so it would bite me again. I stayed up all night, waiting for that ugly, evil creature.

Not the bird-squirrel—Mr. Spoon. ❖

L IFE AT THE ORPHANAGE CONSISTED OF THE SAME OLD routine, day after day. Nothing ever changed—the same room, the same clothes, the same food, the same work, the same games.

One day about ten of us boys got together and went to see Mrs. Dalbert about becoming patrol boys at the Spring Park Elementary School next door to the orphanage. We were very excited about this prospect and wanted to see if she would allow us to get into the program. This was a chance for us to be something special, and Mrs. Cherry, one of the teachers at the school, thought that we should give it a try. Of course, as we anticipated, we got an absolute NO from the "old bag," Mrs. Dalbert.

After returning to school the next day, all of the children had heard that we kids from the orphanage could not become patrol boys and they really made fun of us. I mean, they laughed and made fun of us for days and days and we thought it would never stop.

Later that afternoon all the orphans were gathering out on the school grounds to walk back to the orphanage together. A long line of patrol boys came marching past us, heading for their assigned positions. All we heard as they marched past us is how stupid we were and that we were not smart enough to be patrol boys. This really hurt us and made us very mad, which meant that as soon as we returned to the orphanage a meeting was called to see what could be done about "those stupid patrol boys."

It was decided that we would all walk to school together the next day. If even one of the patrol boys said one word to any of us about being stupid or living in the orphanage, we would just beat the holy hell out of them and that would stop them in their tracks.

The next morning, we all met near the front gate and ate our brown paper bag lunches so they would not get in the way in case we got into a fight. Then we walked in a group of two abreast down the sidewalk toward the school building. Coming upon us were the patrol boys also in long lines of two. The two groups were marching right toward one another and right in the middle of the sidewalk and no one was going to move first. At the last minute, the patrol boys stepped off the sidewalk onto the grass and kept marching.

Without saying a word, we stopped and turned around and looked at them as they marched away. Then one of the boys said that since we won the showdown, it should be us helping all the children across the street; we all agreed. We started running toward the group of patrol boys, and as we reached them, we started pushing them down and confiscating their flags.

We told them that if they did not get their butts back to the school, they'd be sorry and they ran back to the school as fast as they could. We then took their flags, assumed their patrolling positions, and helped all the children cross the street. When we'd finished our duties, we all walked back to the school and marched into Mrs. Drayer's office where all the patrol boys were, just staring out the window at us.

We stacked all the flags neatly against the wall where they belonged and told the patrol boys that we had done the job, and done it right, and that we were not stupid as they said. We warned that if they ever made fun of us again, we would really put them in their place. The teasing started up from time to time, but with another warning or two, it stopped altogether. More importantly, we had proven that the group of us could do the job of "normal" kids, which was something we needed to know for ourselves. ❖

ONE DAY A GENTLEMAN I'D NEVER SEEN BEFORE CAME to the orphanage. He talked with the head office, and they agreed to allow him to come in every other week and teach the children how to do woodworking projects.

I remember the night that I finished my first project, a small table with a Formica top. I was so proud of that table. I looked upon it as though I had created a life. It was absolutely beautiful, and this was the first time in my whole life that the orphanage had allowed me to use my mind to create something.

It had taken me six weeks to complete the project, and I could hardly wait to give my little table to Mrs. Dalbert as a gift. As the table legs were not dry from the clear coating that had been applied, the man asked us to wait until our next session before taking our projects to our dormitories. But I was just so excited and happy I couldn't wait. Besides, my woodworking project was the best one of all (except for this full-sized rowboat some ten-year-old boy was trying to build). I moved my table toward the doorway and waited for the right opportunity to escape with it. When I saw my chance, out the door I went like a flash, running through the darkness with my hands underneath the tabletop, just smiling from ear to ear, as I headed toward the dormitory.

When I reached the dormitory, I placed the beautiful little table beside my bed. I stood there for about ten minutes, just gazing at what I had created with my own hands. Then Mrs. Dalbert entered the room. I pointed at the table and she smiled at me; I felt so proud. She asked me where the other children were, and I told her that they were cleaning up the sawdust and would be coming soon. She walked over to the table and ran her hand across the slick Formica top. "It is very pretty," she told me.

When she touched the table leg, she noticed that the leg was still wet from the clear coating that I had brushed on earlier. She asked me why I had brought the table into the dormitory with the legs still wet. I didn't know what to say, so I just stood there with my head down and did not say anything.

"Were you supposed to bring this home?" she asked.

"No, ma'am," I told her.

Mrs. Dalbert walked over to the little table and, with her foot, kicked it over onto its top. Then she stepped onto each of the small table legs, breaking them off. She then opened the side door and had me throw the little table out into the yard.

After Mrs. Dalbert had left the building and all the other children were asleep, I opened the outside door and went out to get my little table. There was sand stuck all over the legs. I brushed and cried and brushed and cried, but the sand would not come off. I hid the table in my closet. I never returned to the woodshop after that, ever again. About a year later I gave the little table and legs to Mrs. Douglas, my house parent, so she could throw them away. ❖

I WAS WALKING DOWN THE UPSTAIRS HALLWAY HEADED TO MY bedroom, when I decided that I had best tell Mr. and Mrs. Chase, our latest house parents, that I had completed my assigned chores. I believe that I was to clean one of the upstairs bathrooms and sweep the back staircase before going to bed. Living at the orphanage, I had cleaned more toilets and showers than most maids.

I stopped at their door and noticed that it was slightly ajar. I could hear noises coming from their living quarters and had knocked several times, but they did not hear me. Then I called out to them saying that I was done with my chores and I was going to bed. Still there was no response, so I pushed on the door and called to them through the larger opening. Still there was no answer, so I pushed the door open and walked into the little hallway.

When I looked up, there stood this beautiful, naked woman standing in the shower with water running over her face. Her eyes were closed and she did not realize that I was standing there. My mouth fell open to the floor as I just stared at this naked woman with both my eyes open REALLY BIG. After all, this was the first naked woman I had ever seen, except in my wildest dreams, and they were nothing like what I was seeing right now.

Then I heard Mr. Chase yell to Mrs. Chase that he would be back in a moment. As I pulled back out of the doorway, he came around the corner and saw me. I began running down the hallway yelling at the top of my voice, "I did not see anything, I swear! I did not see anything at all!"

I ran down the stairs, full of terror, and went into the closet by the television room. From there I went up into the attic through a hole in the ceiling of the closet. I heard Mr. Chase looking and calling for me for what seemed like hours. He had all the boys looking for me and finally someone found me. They told me that Mr. Chase was not mad at me, so I came down from the attic.

Mr. Chase put all the other boys to bed and then took me out onto the front porch and had a long talk with me. I told Mr. Chase that I did see Mrs. Chase naked and that I would not say anything to the other boys and that I could not remember anything that I saw and that was the truth. I guess he believed me because I didn't get a beating.

As I remember it, I know that I saw this beautiful, naked woman, but I was so scared of what Mr. Chase might have done to me that even to this day, I honestly cannot remember seeing anything at all. That is the God's truth. ❖

NOW I DO REMEMBER *ONE* VACATION THAT WE ORPHANS had while living in The Children's Association in Jacksonville, Florida. I had forgotten all about it. It was a visit to a summer camp named Nunna Hidihi.

I guess that was an Indian name of some sort. Evidently, there was an agreement between the orphanage and the camp officials that the orphans would be allowed to go to the summer camp for one week, but we would have to work to earn our keep. That was fine, except for one thing: we worked the entire time that we were at the camp. I mean, we worked—hard! We raked leaves and pine straw. We cleaned dishes and washed tables after everyone else ate. We even had to eat after everyone else was through. I remember having to clean off the head guy's car because birds had messed on it. I really wanted to go with the other kids and shoot the bow and arrows, but I had to clean that darn car. To this day, I think I would have been very good with a bow and arrows, but I never got the chance to try.

Even as a child, I never minded working for what I got. The work is not what bothered me. What bothered me was the fact that we *always* had to work, that we were *always* ridiculed and

made fun of while all the other normal children got to play—
with no strings attached. By the time we got to have any fun, it
was already too late for us to enjoy ourselves because everybody
already knew that we were not like them, that we were different
in that we did not have any parents, anyone to truly love us.
Therefore, everyone had to service the needs of the normal children first. The orphan always came second, if at all. It was terrible to have to live like that. It was horrible having to walk
around with our heads down, always looking at the ground
because we did not want to look anyone in the eye. I know that
many of the adults who tried to do things for us orphans
thought that they were doing us a great favor, that they were
being kind and generous toward us. On the one hand, they
were, but on the other hand, they were destroying us inside.
They were degrading us as human beings. What if we had been
in wheelchairs? Would they have expected us to rake leaves and
wash dishes? Of course not. They'd have wanted us to feel equal
to all the other kids at the camp.

We orphans were in wheelchairs, folks. You just did not
look hard enough. ❖

THE EXCITEMENT WAS HIGH AS ALL OF THE ORPHANS were herded up into a big circle, which was a common ritual if we were to attend any type of function outside the walls of the orphanage. There was a big celebration to be held at Spring Park Elementary School, and we had practiced for days to enter the sack and three-legged races. We tied our legs together with strips of bamboo and ran the races over and over until we were absolutely positive that we could win.

We walked from the orphanage to the school in our usual two abreast formation, just as we had done for our breakfast, dinner, and supper, day in and day out for years. Of course, everyone attending the celebration was staring at us as we filed onto the schoolyard like a band of young Nazi storm troopers. God, I hated being stared at like that. I felt like nothing more than a "thing" and I know that the other boys did too. To make matters worse, if one of us missed a step or skipped a stride, one of the house parents would run up on you from behind and slap you in the back of the head, sometimes so hard that it would knock you down to the ground, which usually brought laughter from the girls in our class.

Generally, in such times, I would just try and shut out the rest of the world and believe that there was nobody out there except me and the other kids from the orphanage. But that was very hard to do when you were picking yourself up off the ground and heard everyone laughing at you and knowing that you had to face them, especially the girls, the next day in school.

When the races were about to begin, everyone lined up. We knew that all the orphans would be teamed up together for the races and, so, when we lined up at the orphanage to march to the school playground, we paired up with our practice partners. Despite efforts to keep us back, we were good and we knew it and we were going to win! All of the ribbons—red, white, and blue with gold writing on them—were going to be won by us and taken back to the orphanage. We were going to hang them on the wall in the television room for the whole world to see one day.

As the races started, we took the first two or three first-place ribbons with ease. We felt a little bad because some of the kids who were not from the orphanage, who had lost, were crying and being hugged and consoled by their moms and dads. So when the next race began we lagged back a bit and took second place. We had talked it over amongst ourselves and had decided that it was not fair to the other kids because we had practiced so much and were so much quicker.

I lined up for the sack race and was looking for my partner when I heard someone crying. I walked over by the metal swings and saw the matron slapping one of the orphans in the face, over and over, with the burlap sack. He was screaming that his eye was hurt because the sack had popped him in the eye when she hit him the first time. "You little bastard, you could have won first place if you had not been laughing the whole time," she yelled at him. He rolled up into a ball on the ground, but she just kept hitting him over and over with the sack. Finally, Mrs. Cherry, one of the teachers, came running over and grabbed the sack out of her hand and told her to calm down a bit. The boy got up and I took him over to sit down in one of the swings until he could catch his breath.

By now all the boys from the orphanage had gathered by the swings and it was decided that we would not enter any more of the races. Jim Casey picked up the three first-place ribbons and told us that he was going to give them back to the teacher and that they could do all the races over again and give the ribbons to the other kids. I grabbed the ribbons from his hand and told him that we won them fair and square and that the other kids were not going to get them. The other boys agreed with me so I stuck the three ribbons in my back pocket and walked away to get a drink. I walked over by the school building and just stood there, watching the other kids running the different types of races and their moms and dads yelling and screaming for them to win. The kids that would win the race would run up to their parents and the dad or mom would hug and kiss them and would sometimes pick them up and hold them in the air, making them scream for joy.

The boy that had been beaten with the sack came over and sat on the ground beside me. "They are winning all the ribbons now," he said. "So what," I told him. "It's not fair," he said in a low whisper. I reached in my pocket and took out one of the ribbons and threw it at him. "Here's your damn ribbon," I told him. He picked up the ribbon and tore it in half, longways, and threw it on the ground beside him. "That's not what I mean," he yelled at me. I picked up the two pieces of ribbon and placed them in my pocket. The boy stood up, walked behind me, and started banging his head against the red brick wall of the school building as hard as he could. I grabbed him by the collar of the shirt, pulling him away from the wall, and said, "What the heck is wrong with you?" "Nobody cares if we win or lose," he said while walking away, rubbing his eyes.

I stood there for about ten minutes just looking at all the other kids from the orphanage watching the other kids win all the ribbons. I sat down on the ground and took all the ribbons out of my pocket and tore them in half, longways. Then I went underneath the school building through a special hole that only we orphans knew about—a special place where we used to hide when we got beaten or ran away, a place that no one in the world knew about except us. We had a deep hole dug in the sand for a bed and we had an old blanket to keep warm when it was cold, and some old wooden fruit boxes to keep our stuff in. I sat there for the longest time just wishing that I would never have to go back to school ever again.

The next thing I remember I was in Juvenile Hall locked in this big, wire cage. The next morning I was taken downstairs before the judge. He asked me why I had done what I did. I told him I did not know what he was talking about. He told me that I had broken out about fifteen of the school's windows with large rocks and was screaming as loud as I could, over and over and over, "YOU LOSE, YOU LOSE, YOU LOSE!"

I was taken to see some type of special doctor who asked me what was wrong with me. I told him about the races at the school and that we should have gotten the ribbons, and I told him about my friend who got beaten with the sack. He got up from his big brown chair and walked out of his office for a minute. When he came back, he handed me a peanut butter log and squeezed the back of my neck. "What's wrong with me?" I asked him. He patted me on the arm and pulled me out of the chair. He bent down on his knee and held me by both my arms, looked me in the eye, and said, "There's something wrong here, boy, and it's not with you, and don't you ever forget that."

He took me back to Juvenile Hall and he went in the office to talk to the judge for a long time. When he came out, he put me in his car and took me for an ice cream before returning me to the orphanage.

After that the orphanage people never called me a "bastard" again. They just called me "the nut case." ❖

P EER PRESSURE? I BET MOST PEOPLE DO NOT REALIZE THAT peer pressure is a sport, more fun in an orphanage than throwing Christians to the lions was to the Romans, and it was all legal, too. Well, sort of. All that's needed for an event like this is twenty or thirty little orphan children, ones about whom nobody gives a damn. That way, there is no one to complain to the organizers. Then, a really secluded spot needs to be found, just like the one at The Children's Association in Jacksonville, Florida: an area that is completely fenced and hidden by lots of thick bamboo and trees. No one else can see what is going on. Now the stage is set for some real blood-and-guts action.

For years, it was the policy of many of the house parents at The Children's Association to use the children against one another as a form of control and discipline. To escape this severe and cruel treatment is one of the many reasons that I kept running away from the orphanage.

About every week or so, all of the children would be told to line up and to march out into a field located behind the boys' building. We were then herded into a large circle. We knew very well what was about to happen to us. We just did not know to whom it was going to happen.

Many of the smaller kids started crying as soon as we got into the circle. Some tried to make a break for it and run toward the bamboo clumps in order to hide, but they were always caught, slapped on the head a few times, and then dragged back into the circle. The adults would ask each child if he or she was having any problems with any of the other children. Most of the children would not say anything at all. They would just shake their heads back and forth.

If there appeared to be any type of dispute, those two children would be placed in the center of the circle and forced to fight until blood was drawn—generally, lots of blood. Size or age made no difference whatsoever. The time or length of the beating did not matter. Remember, this event was considered a sport, not child abuse. It was absolutely disgraceful. At times, it was horrifying. Sometimes the bigger boys would beat the smaller boys until the smaller ones were not recognizable; that is how bloody it was sometimes.

I will always remember how these "games" reminded me of the gladiators on television: the sadness of the losers, yet the pride of the victors and the honor bestowed upon them as they were congratulated by the adults. I will never forget the screaming or the yelling, the jumping up and down, and all the pushing and shoving—all that fear on the faces of those small children, and the eyes of those crazed with excitement. This is a very terrible story to tell, but what was even more terrible was to be there and to feel it happening.

We knew that we had to be strong or we were as good as dead. Most of the time, I just stood there. I kept my mouth shut and said nothing at all. I mean nothing. I just watched the others' faces, especially the looks in their eyes. I just held my breath and waited to see if I was going to be the chosen one. Sometimes we were very lucky and the adults would bring out boxing gloves. Using gloves meant that our faces did not get messed up so badly. I never liked the boxing gloves myself, though, because when using them, we had to beat on each other that much longer in order to draw blood.

As I was about ten or eleven at that time, I never was beaten on very much. When I was called into the arena, even most of the older boys stayed away from me. I had a reputation for being a very good kicker. If I kicked one of the others in the right place, he would talk really squeaky for about a week. So many of the older boys tried to stay away from me. They did not want to take a chance on being embarrassed in front of the other boys or the adults so, generally, they left me alone.

When I did get picked to enter the arena, my opponent always stayed as far away from me as possible. He would never attack me head on. Instead, he would just keep slapping me in the face until my nose got bloody.

In time, I learned a trick—my big secret. I could save a lot of beating time if I just left my face open to the slaps. After ten or fifteen good pops to the side of the face, my nose would start to bleed. On the next slap, I would fall to the ground and roll into a tight ball, leaving me open for attack by my opponent. While he was on top of me, I would be smearing the blood from my nose all over my face and neck. When I unrolled from my tight ball with my blood-curdling scream, sucking large blood bubbles in and out of my nose, all anyone could see was this MONSTER from HELL.

Things really got quiet around there after that episode. ❖

THE CLOSETS AT THE ORPHANAGE WERE ALWAYS SCARY places. Many a two- or three-day period we spent locked away in those dark, scary closets without any food, water, or a place to go to the bathroom. Many a time as an orphan boy, I lay in the dark corner of those closets with blood dripping from my head wounds from the beatings that I had received from the house parents, because I had not waxed the checkerboard floor correctly, left the soap sock in the sink, or forgot to flush the toilet. Even today I will still not enter a dark closet without the aid of a flashlight or a lamp in hand.

It is true that we did get into much mischief as little boys while living at the orphanage. There was never anything for us to do. There were never any toys for us to play with so we made things out of sticks and cans, and we would build army forts under the ground, in which we hid for hours at a time, just to feel safe.

One day I went into the main dining room building where Mrs. Dalbert lived. As I entered I could not see her anywhere, so I walked over to the big opening leading down to her bedroom. I stopped at the entrance of the long hallway and just looked for a long time. As I stood there I noticed the (always) locked closet, next to the little bathroom, was slightly ajar, so I took one big, giant step over toward it and pushed the door open. This was the only closet that we had never been locked in and we never could figure out why. But as I walked slowly into the small, long closet I finally understood why.

For as far as my eyes could see, there were presents and toys that went on forever and ever, all the way from the floor to the ceiling. There were roller skates, and balls, and lots of gloves and bats. There were little cars, big trucks that could carry dirt, and airplanes—some that could really fly and that used real gas to make them go way up in the air and go far away. There were lots of dolls and girl things, too, like playhouses and little bitty clothes.

I stood for the longest time, wondering why we did not have anything to play with and why Mrs. Dalbert had all this good stuff to play with, whenever she wanted to. As I stood there amazed at what I had found, I started to play, real quiet-like, with some of the little green toy soldiers. I lined them up for battle and they fought each other and some of them got killed when they fell off the wooden shelf onto the floor. But I made them come back to life again so I could play with them over and over again.

"What the damn hell are you doing in there," yelled Mrs. Dalbert. "Nothing," I said to her as I placed my hands behind my back. "Put your damn hand in the doorway," she told me. "That's gonna hurt me again," I said. Mrs. Dalbert had slammed my hand in the doorway once before when she caught me looking into the kitchen pantry and taking one of her special boxes of raisins because I was hungry. "Put your damn hand in the damn doorway," she demanded, gritting her teeth. "I can't, Mother Dalbert. It just hurts too bad when you do that," I said again, turning my eyes down toward the floor. Mrs. Dalbert grabbed me by the shirt collar and slammed my face into the bottom shelf where the toys were stacked, knocking them everywhere and crashing me to the floor. "Keep your little ass right there until I get the damn polo paddle, do you understand me?" she said. "Yes, ma'am," I said back to her.

After she left I started picking up the green toy soldiers that had fallen onto the floor when she slammed my face into the shelves. I noticed that some of them had blood on them. I started picking them up as fast as I could and started placing them into my pants pocket so I could play with them later.

When Mrs. Dalbert returned I told her that my teeth were loose and that I was hurting real, real bad in my face. Her eyes got real big and she hit me one time on the hand with the polo paddle really hard and told me to get my little ass back to the boys' building and get up to my room and stay there for the rest of the day.

When I got back to the dormitory I told all the other boys about all the toys and presents that were in the closet and then I went to the bathroom and wet some toilet paper and put it into my mouth so the bleeding would stop and my teeth would not move around anymore.

Then I went to my room, like I was told, and played war with the five bloody soldiers that I took from the closet by Mrs. Dalbert's bedroom. But they didn't want to play very long because they were already hurt and real bloody, so I just cried and went to sleep until the next day. ❖

"COME ON AND GET YOUR BUTT UP," I HEARD, AS someone shook me awake from a deep sleep. "What's going on?" I said, rubbing my swollen eyes. "We are going to break into Spring Park and get some money and then we can run away from this orphanage," the redheaded boy said to me. "I'm tired," I told him, as I rolled back over and faced the wall.

But within minutes, five or six of us boys were dressed and headed out into the darkness, sneaking toward the Spring Park Elementary School, just on the other side of the large chain-link fences that surrounded the orphanage.

"Darn it. Someone locked the window I left open in my classroom," said the redheaded boy as he picked up a large rock and hit the window, breaking it into a million pieces.

Seconds later we were traveling down the long, dark hallway of the school, going from classroom to classroom, looking in every teacher's desk for money and candy. Finally we reached Mrs. Drayer's office but the door was locked. We knew we had to get into the principal's office as that was where all the milk money was kept for the cafeteria. That is what this was all about—getting a big haul of cash that would allow us to run away from the orphanage and find a good place to live with a nice man and woman. Someone who would hug and kiss us all the time and be good and kind to us, just like we saw on the little black-and-white television at the orphanage.

Within minutes one of the boys ran back down the long, dark hallway where we had entered, ran around the entire school building, broke out a window in the office, climbed in, and opened the large wooden door, allowing us to enter into Mrs. Drayer's office.

As we walked around the office, searching every nook and cranny for money, I saw a large fish aquarium beside the entrance door. I just stood there for the longest time looking at the fish swimming back and forth and back and forth. All of a sudden one of the boys dumped a large bottle of ink into the aquarium. "Don't do that," I said to him. "You'll kill them!" I yelled as loud as I could. The boy laughed and continued to dump the bottle of ink into the large fish tank. I reached over and slapped the bottle of ink, as hard as I could, from his hand, causing the ink to spray all over the windows, wall, and the other boys as well as myself.

"I've got the money," yelled Jim Casey and then everyone started climbing out the office window and running back across the large schoolyard toward the orphanage fence. I looked over at the big tank and knew that all the fish were going to choke to death.

I removed my white tee shirt and dipped it into the tank, hoping that it would take the ink out of the water so that the little fish would not die. But it did not work. I grabbed a large brown envelope off the desk and caught the fish and put them into the envelope and ran down to the girls' bathroom, where I dumped the fish into the toilet where they could have clean water to drink and I left the school.

When I returned to the orphanage the other boys had already run away and I had no idea where they had gone. I ran over to the old Spanish house, which had been deserted years before, a place where we orphans slept when we ran away and had nowhere else to go, but they were nowhere to be found.

I was cold, lonely, and scared, and I was covered in ink from head to toe. I knew that I was going to get the beating of my life when the orphanage people found out what we had done at the school. I returned to the school building to check on the fish, which were still swimming around in the toilet. I lay down on the floor, next to the fish, and fell asleep. The next thing I knew I was awakened by the janitor and the police, who took me to Juvenile Hall in downtown Jacksonville, Florida, to see Judge Davis.

I tried to tell the big judge in the long black coat that I loved the fish and that I did not hurt them, but he called me "a little liar" and a "worthless delinquent." The judge made me stay in a small wire cage for two weeks for pouring ink into the fish tank and for trying to flush them down the toilet. Then he sent me back to the orphanage where they locked me in a closet, by the television room, from Friday night until Sunday afternoon without any food or water.

I really did love those fish. ❖

THERE WAS A TIME AT THE CHILDREN'S ASSOCIATION when we children were receiving beatings almost on a daily basis, especially when we were being taken care of by Mr. and Mrs. Spoon. Mr. Spoon was a very cruel and harsh man who had no compassion in his heart for children—none whatsoever. This man was one mean son of a bitch. Sorry, but there can be no other words to describe a man like him.

No matter how small the infractions, the children would be taken into the sewing room and beaten within an inch of their lives—and I mean within an inch of their lives.

Evidently, he got some form of joy out of beating small children. One could see it in his eyes and in the smile on his face. As I look back on these beatings today, I think it was a sexual thing with him. Of course, we did not know about those types of things back then. After all, we were only young boys.

Finally, we children could take no more of his beatings. We talked about running away together, but decided that it would be better to beat him to death before he killed one of us. We all got together one night and discussed what would be the best thing to do. I will never forget my little heart beating really fast as we talked about killing him and how we would do it. I will never forget feeling my heart beating on the side of my neck. "THUMP, THUMP, THUMP," it went. I even got dizzy, I was so scared. I didn't want to hurt anybody, but I was not going to say anything because I was not going to be the chicken.

On Saturday morning, Mr. Spoon called all of us to the front porch and told us all to line up at the door of the sewing room. After we lined up, Mr. Spoon went into the room and closed the door. We heard him sliding the big table around so that we could lie across it while he beat us. None of us kids even spoke a word; we just stood there looking at one another and shaking, all wondering if we could really kill this evil man before he killed us. But no one moved or did anything. We just stood there, scared and horrified.

Then the door opened, and Mr. Spoon called the first boy into the room and closed the door behind him. It was really quiet for about a minute; then we heard the boy start to scream and yell as he was being beaten. The group of boys in line started backing up from the sewing room door and backing down the hallway toward the television room. The boy being beaten just kept on yelling and screaming, hollering for us—by name—to come in and help him. Then one of the older boys yelled, "Let's go," and we all started running toward the sewing room, yelling and screaming at the top of our voices.

As the door opened, all of the boys grabbed Mr. Spoon, threw him to the floor, and began beating him with their fists, with ping-pong paddles, with anything that they could get a hold of. I grabbed a large pair of scissors and ran toward Mr. Spoon, trying to stab him, but I could not get close enough to wound him because of all the boys who were beating on him. They were yelling over and over, "Kill him! Kill him! Kill him!" I just stood there, looking and yelling along with them to kill him, and I kept stabbing that damn sewing table over and over and over as hard as I could. I must have stabbed that table a hundred thousand times. Then he did not move anymore, and we closed the sewing room door and left him for dead. Well, we did not kill Mr. Spoon, but we thought we had—and we wished we had. We watched them cart him off to the hospital, where he was treated for many deserved injuries. I never saw him again after that day, and I thank God for small miracles. I thank God for giving us enough nine-, ten-, eleven-, and twelve-year-old little balls to save our own lives. ❖

AT TEN YEARS OLD I COULD NOT FIGURE OUT WHAT IT was that this Elvis Presley guy had that the rest of us boys did not have. I mean he had a head, two arms, and two legs, just like the rest of us. Whatever it was he had hidden away must have been pretty darn good because he had every young girl at the orphanage wrapped around his little finger.

About nine o'clock one Saturday morning I decided to ask Jim Casey, one of the older boys, what it was that made this Elvis guy so special. He told me that it was Elvis's wavy hair and the way he moved his body.

About a half an hour later all the boys in the orphanage were called to the main dining room and told that we were all going to downtown Jacksonville, Florida, to get a new pair of Buster Brown shoes and a haircut. That is when I got this big idea, which hit me like a ton of bricks. If the Elvis haircut was the big secret, then that's what I was going to get.

All the way to town that was all I talked about. The Elvis haircut that I was going to get. I told everybody, including the matron from the orphanage who was taking us to town, that I was going to look just like Elvis Presley and that I would learn to move around just like he did and that I would be rich and famous one day, just like him.

We got our new Buster Brown shoes and I was very proud as I walked around the store. They shined really, really good and I liked looking at the bones in my feet through that special x-ray machine that they had in the shoe store that made your bones look green.

I could hardly wait for my new haircut, and now that I had my new Buster Brown shoes I would be very happy to go back to the orphanage and practice being like Elvis.

We finally arrived at the big barbershop where they cut our hair for free because we were orphans. I ran up to one of the barber chairs and climbed up onto the board that he put across the arms to make me sit up higher. I looked at the man and said, "I want an Elvis haircut. Can you make my hair like Elvis?" I asked him, with a great big smile on my face. "Let's just see what we can do for you, little man," he said.

I was so happy when he started to cut my hair. Just as he started to cut my hair the matron motioned for him to come over to where she was standing. She whispered something into his ear and then he shook his head, like he was telling her, "No." She walked over to another man sitting in the office chair and spoke to him. Then the little man walked over and said something to the man who was cutting my hair. The next thing I knew, the man who was cutting my hair told me that they were not allowed to give us Elvis haircuts. I saw him put this comb thing onto the end of the clippers and then I saw all my hair falling onto the floor.

When he finished shaving off all my hair and made me smell real good with this powder, he handed me a nickel and told me to go outside to the candy machine and buy myself a candy bar, but I handed him the nickel back and told him that I was not hungry. "I'm so sorry, baby," he said, as I climbed out of his barber chair. "I am not a baby," I said, as I wiped the tears from my eyes. I sat down on the floor and brushed the hair off my new Buster Brown shoes so they would stay shiny and new.

I got up off the floor and brushed off my short pants and walked toward the door. The matron was smiling at me sort of funny. The man who had cut my hair walked over to her and said to her, "You are a damn bitch, lady." She yelled at him and walked toward the office. The man hit the wall with his hand and then walked outside where he stood against the brick wall, smoking a cigarette. I walked outside and stood beside him. He smiled at me, then patted me on the top of my bald head. I looked up at him and said, "Do you know if Elvis has green bones?" ❖

ONE NIGHT IN DECEMBER, ALL OF THE CHILDREN HAD gone to bed and things were just starting to get quiet. At about ten o'clock that evening, several of the boys came to my room and asked me if I wanted to sneak downstairs to see the great big Christmas tree that had been donated to the orphanage. Of course, I was more than willing to go with them. After all, this was the very first Christmas tree that we ever had at the orphanage.

The five of us traveled from room to room until all the boys that could be trusted were rounded up. Slowly we all made our way down the long, dark hallway to the stairs. Then down the creaky stairway we traveled. At last, we reached the living room doorway.

All of a sudden there was a loud noise at the far end of the downstairs hallway. All eleven or twelve of us boys panicked. We all made a mad dash for the back staircase and headed for our separate bedrooms upstairs. It sounded like a herd of horses, running across the plains. Laughing and yelling, pushing and shoving. A herd of little boys slipping and falling all over one another. However, the house parents did not agree.

They went from room to room, screaming and yelling at all the boys.

Of course, we acted like we were all sleeping and did not know what was happening. Several minutes later I heard one of the boys being slapped around, so I decided to go to sleep. I never did learn who it was they caught, but I did learn what happened. When we all decided to sneak downstairs, one of the boys stopped to use the bathroom. When he came back out of the bathroom, we were all gone. For some stupid reason, he decided to go down the staircase near the house parents' bedroom. What a fool! He was that strange noise that we heard at the far end of the downstairs hallway.

At about one o'clock in the morning I was awakened again, this time by Dean Whitcomb. Dean and I traveled from room to room, waking up about five other boys. The seven of us headed back down the stairs to the living room door. When we entered the living room, we slowly closed the door and turned on the light. There stood this magnificent Christmas tree right in the middle of the living room floor. It was a beauty. Boy, did that thing smell good. We had never smelled anything like it before.

We all gathered around the Christmas tree and just kept smelling and smelling. I kept touching the limbs and noticing that they would stick into you. But that was all right, it still smelled really good. We were all really excited. Our first Christmas tree and it was all ours.

Well, not really our first Christmas tree. We had a Christmas tree every year, but it was over at the office where Mrs. Dalbert slept. It was down a long hallway and we were not allowed to go near it. It was in the piano room at the end of the fifty-foot hallway. It was always white with blue lights and blue balls. That's all I ever knew about it. I don't think any of us children ever saw it up close.

Anyway, to the left of the living room door was the old Philco radio. It was a big old thing, almost as tall as me. One of the boys bumped into the radio and we heard the knob click on. I reached over and turned the knob as far to the right as it would go. I thought that I had turned the radio off. However, what I did not realize was that I had turned the radio up to full volume. Of course there was no sound, because the radio tubes had to warm up first. We did not know that, so we continued on with the business at hand. Then we decided to venture out onto the front porch and see if we could see any babes across the street at the girls' dormitory.

As we opened the glass outside door, going out onto the front porch, that damn Philco came on. FULL BLAST. I mean LOUD. VERY LOUD. Scared the holy hell out of us kids. Jesus, there were orphans running north, south, east, and west. Not to mention up and down. It was one heck of a mess. I tried to close the glass door, but it would not close—there was a foot stuck in the doorway. So I just let it go and I turned around to run. As I did the lights went off and there was nothing but total darkness.

The next thing I remember was that there was a big crash. Then there were little green pine needles sticking all over me. Then the light came on. It was the house parent. He was screaming at me at the top of his voice. He walked over to the Philco and jerked the plug out of the wall. I slowly climbed out of the Christmas tree, which was now lying on its side. I tried to stand it back up, but it just kept falling over. So I just stood there holding it in my hand. The man yelled at me to "just throw the damn thing down" and to get a broom. The big crash that we heard was the boxes of decorations hitting the floor and breaking into a thousand million pieces.

When I returned with the broom I was instructed to sweep up all the broken glass and the needles from the tree. As I swept the floor, he asked me who all was in the living room with me. I told him that I did not know because it was dark when I arrived. He grabbed the broom out of my hand and started stabbing my feet with the broom bristles. I just kept jumping up and down so that it didn't hurt so badly. Then he threw the broom down and walked out of the room.

I continued sweeping up the broken glass. I noticed that the beautiful Christmas tree had several broken limbs. I tried to make them straight, but one of them broke off. I smelled the limb and hid it behind the Philco. I cleaned up all the glass and needles and put them in the dustpan, then took them to the back room where the garbage was kept. I walked up the stairs to my room and got into bed. Then the man came in and asked me if I had cleaned up the living room. I told him that I had.

He left the room and started yelling at some of the other boys. One of the older boys, Jack, was helping him. Jack came into my room and told me that I was a retard, just like the rest of the boys in the home. About a half an hour later, Mrs. Dalbert showed up. She told me to go downstairs and wait in the living room. When I arrived in the living room, the man grabbed me by the pajama top and told me to look for more glass. I looked and looked, but I could not find any. Then he told me that if he found any glass that he would make me eat it. He looked everywhere, but there was no glass to be found. Thank God for that! All those years of cleaning paid off.

Then he moved the Philco. There was one big piece of red glass. He just looked at me and started shaking his finger, up and down real slow, pointing at the piece of glass. I just stood there. He reached down and picked up the glass and handed it to me. I took the glass and held it in my hand. I just stared at him. I was not even afraid and I don't know why.

"I SAID PUT IT IN YOUR MOUTH!" he yelled.

Then he started hitting me with the broken Christmas tree branch. I raised the broken glass to my lips and bit off a piece with my teeth. I never let my eyes leave his. He knew I hated him for what he was doing. Just as I started to chew, he told me to go to the bathroom and spit out the glass and wash my mouth out with the soap sock.

The next day that same man bought us five whole bags of marshmallows, which we roasted over our beautiful, burning Christmas tree. Believe it or not, that was the best Christmas we ever had, because we had never had marshmallows before. ❖

ONE SUNDAY, WE WERE ALL LOADED ONTO THE CHURCH bus in order to attend a Sunday supper being held at the Swain Memorial Methodist Church in Jacksonville. Even today I can remember these Sunday Methodist Youth Fellowship meetings (MYF), as they had a big impact on my life as a child in the orphanage, and maybe as a grown adult.

This was one of the only times I can remember when we orphans were allowed to be kids. We would eat supper in the church basement and then we would all play volleyball for several hours. It felt good to run free and it was wonderful not to have someone from the orphanage breathing down your neck, slapping you upside the head, or telling you that you were stupid or worthless.

If I have any good feelings in my heart toward the Methodist church community, this one Sunday evening fellowship meeting would be what stands out in my mind as the most good, kind, friendly, and loving of all the things that the church ever did for us children.

This one Sunday evening one of the members of the church asked us orphans if we would like to become Boy Scouts and

155

join the troop at the church. We were flabbergasted and could not believe that such a thing could ever come true. We told them that the orphanage would never allow us to do anything like that. After all, we boys had been denied becoming patrol boys at our school because the orphanage had told the school principal that we were not smart enough to follow directions. The man just stood there looking at us, and he could see how excited we were. He told us that he would talk with the orphanage and see what could be done. Every night I prayed to God, asking him to allow this miracle to happen. I would walk around all day long, every day, saying the different books of the Bible and asking God to give us this one chance to become somebody important. But hours turned into days, and days turned into weeks, and weeks turned into months, and we never heard anything at all, and after a while none of the boys even mentioned it again. But I never did stop thinking about it and I never stopped praying about wanting to wear that uniform or becoming somebody as important as a Boy Scout.

Wayne Evers and I were taking turns pushing one another around on a rigged-up old skateboard on the concrete slab behind the boys' dormitory, when we looked up and saw the man from the church walking toward us, waving his hand in the air. "Are there any want-to-be Boy Scouts here?" he yelled. We all stood up and watched him as he made his way to where we were standing. When he approached us he said, "Well, fellows, I have brought your new uniforms. All of you are now Boy Scouts of America, and I salute you." We all ran up and started hugging the man and thanking him for what he had done. I ran toward the bamboo, where other boys were building forts and playing cowboys and Indians, and told them the good news. "It is Gospel, it is Gospel, we are Boy Scouts!" I yelled as loud as I could at the other boys. God, that was a happy day in my life.

We followed the man over to the screened-in dining room porch and there lay fifteen or twenty uniforms. I will never forget the color and how good they smelled for as long as I live. I picked up one of the uniform shirts and held it up to myself, then I walked over to the door to the infirmary and smiled as I looked at myself in the reflection of the glass window. "You look good," I said out loud. "Now you are going to be somebody important," I thought to myself. I walked over to the man and asked him if I could please try on the shirt. He took the shirt from me, unbuttoned it, and handed it back to me. I slipped it on and very carefully picked up the beautiful scarf that was lying on the chair. I placed the scarf around my neck and slid the metal clip onto the scarf. All the other boys started putting on their shirts and scarves. We were all so proud and we walked around and around the porch just smiling at each other and looking real proud and all.

We were told at church the following Sunday morning that we were lucky, because the first thing we were going to get to do was go on a camping trip for a whole week. When we returned to the orphanage, I studied tying knots day and night just to get my first merit badge before going on the camping trip. I was given my first badge but did not have a way to sew it on my uniform, so I glued it to my uniform with model airplane glue and off we went to the great outdoors for our camping trip.

When we arrived, there were all kinds of strange boys all over the place. I had never seen any of these boys at our church before. I asked the leader where all these boys came from. "Well this is like a Jamboree. Boys from all over get together and camp for a week," he said. Well, all day long we kids from the orphanage knew something was not right with these other Boy Scouts. They kept looking at us funny and flipping their four fingers off the end of their noses, whatever that meant. But we just sort of ignored it so we would not get into trouble. Later that night we had a campfire and told scary stories with just our own little group from the church and it was lots of fun.

Then it was time to go to bed and we went to our tents, which we had set up when we first made it to our camp. As I went to my tent I was repeating over and over "a scout is trustworthy, loyal, friendly, courteous, kind, obedient, cheerful, thrifty . . ." and as I got into my sleeping bag I felt something funny and wet inside, which scared me. I jumped out of my sleeping bag and ran over to the other tent and as I walked in I saw other boys from the orphanage getting out of their sleeping bags with yellow stuff dripping off their shorts. "Hope you orphans like eggs," yelled someone from down the aisle of tents.

This really upset the boys from the orphanage and it took quite a while for the scoutmaster to get everyone settled down. He finally got it through our heads that a scout must always be trustworthy, loyal, friendly, courteous, kind, and all that good stuff, so we went to bed after cleaning up the best we could. Later that night, I guess about four in the morning, a bunch of scouts ran into our dark tent and started dumping their canteens of water onto our sleeping bags and then ran out into the darkness. I tried to calm the other boys and remind them that we were scouts and that scouts should always be friendly, no matter what.

I got up and started to dress but could not find my shirt. I looked all over but it was gone. I walked outside the tent and saw three or four men come in with a truck and start unloading flats of eggs onto a large table. There were tons of eggs, and I mean thousands, all stacked on top of one another. I walked over to look at all those eggs and stood next to the fire to stay warm. I looked down and as I did I saw my shirt burning in the campfire. I jerked it out and tried to put out the fire by stomping on it, but it was too late. I looked for my badge but it was not on the shirt. I walked back to the tent and told the other boys that someone had thrown my shirt into the camp-fire. Then I heard someone yell out, "Looking for that stupid badge, creeps?"

That was the final straw; the hornet's nest had been poked for the last time. Within minutes there were more than 3,000 eggs destroyed at that camp, all by orphan hands, not to mention five tents, two canoes, and the pride of ten or twenty non-orphan Boy Scouts. I remember smiling as we were being told that we were not worthy of being Boy Scouts and that we were being kicked out of the scout troop.

We were returned to the orphanage later that day, not feeling very trustworthy, friendly, loyal, kind, obedient, thrifty, clean, or reverent. However, we did feel "CHEERFUL" and "BRAVE." ❖

ONE NIGHT, SEVERAL OF THE BOYS CAME TO MY ROOM and asked me if I wanted to smoke a cigarette with them. I told them I did not want to smoke, but they insisted that I come with them and watch how it was done.

We exited the boys' building through the upstairs window in the bedroom that Wayne Evers and I shared. Then we climbed down an old oak tree right outside of the window until we reached the ground. We walked very slowly around the building to the heater room that was located out back between the boys' building and the orphanage office.

At that very spot was where some of the office workers left their cars at night, cars with hundreds of half-smoked cigarette butts. The boys would open the car doors and empty the ashtrays into a bag that they had hidden. Later they would smoke the cigarette butts.

All of a sudden several of the boys grabbed me from behind and started pulling my pajamas off until I was totally naked. Then they took my pajamas and tied my hands and feet so that I could not walk or run. They carried me across the street to the girls' dormitory and opened the glass door at the end of the hallway. Then they grabbed me by the arms and feet and slid me as far down the hallway toward the girls' bedrooms as I would slide.

Then the ten or twelve boys started yelling as loud as they could before running out the door and back to the boys' building. As it was one o'clock in the morning, every girl in the orphanage as well as the matron came running out of her bedroom to see what was happening—and there I lay, naked as a jaybird.

The matron started yelling at all the girls to get back into their bedrooms and not to look at this naked man. She was screaming, "OH, MY GOD, a naked man! OH, MY GOD!" Over and over and over she screamed, and I just lay there, hoping that nobody would see my "thing."

Then the matron came up to me and told me that all us boys needed some "mental help." I told her that all I needed was some pajamas, and she kicked me in the back and told me to be quiet. Then Susan Adams came running with a towel that she gave to the matron, who covered me up. I saw Susan Adams looking at me where she was not supposed to be looking, and I know she told all the other girls because they all laughed at me for weeks. But that was all right, because Susan Adams let me kiss her on the cheek the next time we played Post Office.

So, to all you boys who did this to me, stick that in your pipe and smoke it! Ha, ha! ❖

TIRED OF BEING HARSHLY PUNISHED AND WONDERING what the outside world was like, I would run away from the orphanage upon occasion. Usually, I would just hide out for the day and end up back where I started. At the age of twelve, however, I had determined that I was going to leave for good. I had had it.

This time I was leaving because the matron had told one of the smaller boys that she was going to "cut his wee-wee off" with the scissors if he wet the bed one more time.

Well, the next morning when I got up and went in to use the bathroom, I found David sitting in the corner of the shower, sobbing his eyes out, and I could not get him to stop. I walked to his bedroom and found that his sheets had been pulled off his bed and that they were burnt. I ran back to the bathroom and asked him how his sheet got burnt like that. He told me that he had wet the bed and that he had gone into one of the older boys' lockers and had taken some matches that they used for smoking cigarette butts that they stole out of the office ladies' cars. He had tried to dry the sheets with the matches, but one sheet caught on fire and he had to stick it into the toilet to get the fire to go out.

I knew that this four-year-old kid was as good as dead when they found out what he had done. I told him to go to his room and get his clothes and shoes on because we were going to go away and that I would make sure that he would never be beaten or have his wee-wee cut off for wetting the bed. Within fifteen minutes we had scaled down the oak tree outside my bedroom window and were headed down the road to who knows where.

We got several rides from different people and we finally made it to St. Augustine, Florida, where I managed to steal some apples from a store so we could eat. I made sure that he did not see me steal the apples because I did not want him to grow up and become "a no-good thief" like me, which is what the orphanage always called me after I was caught fishing in a man's goldfish pond and eating pears off his fruit trees.

We walked around for several hours wondering where to go. This man came walking up to us and asked us if we wanted a job selling magazines. I told him I would sell his magazines if my friend could stay with me, and he said that was okay. He took us to this big street with lots of nice homes and told us to go from door to door and let them fill out the papers. They would give us some money and we were to bring the money back to him at his car.

Most of the people got real mad at me for coming up to their house and for knocking on their door. I did not like them yelling at me like that. So I told the man that I did not want to sell his magazines anymore. He put us in his car and took us for a hamburger and said that he would take us to a new place to sell the magazines where the people would not be so mean to us.

After he dropped us off in the new place, I decided to try something new. So I took a piece of paper and wrote a note telling the people that I was deaf and dumb. Then I would walk up to their house and I would knock. When they came to the door I would hand them the note that I had written and talk while biting my tongue, sounding like I was nuts or something. That made me sound like I was really stupid, and then I would hand them the paper for the magazines. I never did get yelled at doing it that way.

Within several hours I had collected almost eighty dollars and the man started hugging me when we got back to his car. He asked me if we wanted to go to Miami with him. That we could make lots of money in Miami and that we could stay in a big hotel. So off we went, just the three of us.

We arrived in Miami late that night and he got the three of us a room at the Hawaiian Isles Motel. I will never forget the name of that fancy place. It even had a swimming pool, and it was where all the rich people stayed, he told us. But I did not see any fancy people staying there. Just plain people like us.

We made Troy lots of money every day, but he would never give us any of it. All we ever got to eat was one hamburger at nighttime, when we turned in our money. I did take some of the money to buy us a Coke, and I did buy us an ice cream one time from a man on a bicycle with a freezer on the front.

Every day we would get really hungry and could hardly wait to get back to the motel to get our hamburger. One day we had made lots of money, so I took my friend David into a drugstore and we bought a sandwich and a bunch of candy bars. Boy, was Troy mad when he found out what we had done. He pushed me down on the ground and then he slapped little David across the face as hard as he could.

Late that night I woke David up and we sneaked out of the room and ran away again. We lived on the beach for two days without anything to eat. Finally I went to a restaurant and asked a man for some money so I could call the orphanage and tell them where we were. He gave me a dollar and I walked into the back room to use the phone. I called the operator and asked her for the number of the orphanage in Jacksonville, but she did not know what I was talking about and told me to hold on.

While I was waiting on her I saw a big freezer right next to me. I reached over and opened one of the big white doors. Inside were hundreds of hamburger patties, with paper between each one. I hung up the phone and grabbed about ten of the hamburgers and put them down the front of my pants, which did not feel real good after about a minute. I walked out of the restaurant really fast and stiff-legged, and we headed back down to the beach.

When we arrived back down on the beach we started gathering firewood so we could make a fire and cook the hamburgers. We were really hungry and our stomachs were hurting really bad. After we got a light for the fire we tried to hold the hamburgers over the heat but it was just too hot and we could not hold on to them. I decided to walk up to the back of the motel to see if I could find anything to cook on, like a piece of metal, but there was nothing there to use. I looked around and found a piece of glass and decided to cut the window screen out of the motel window and use it as a cooking thing to lay over the fire and put the hamburgers on.

Well, the screen melted and the hamburgers fell into the fire. We grabbed as much of the uncooked meat as we could and we ate what we could save, even though it had sand all over it. But most of it was not cooked, so we just covered it up and decided to make that phone call to the orphanage.

David and I walked down the beach and we discussed going way out into the water where maybe we would drown or be pulled way out into the ocean where a big ship might pick us up and take us way across to the other side of the world. But I was too afraid to do that, so we just kept walking.

We made our way up to this great, big hotel with lots of lights. We walked around to the front of the building where all these people were yelling and screaming at one another. Then everything got real still and quiet.

We just stood there with lots of other people who were watching as this really pretty lady with diamonds all over her and a big fur coat came walking out of the hotel and got into this big fancy car.

Then everyone started talking and yelling again. I saw these men with cameras taking pictures of the car. I told David that this was a movie about that big fancy car and that it would probably be on television one day.

I had never seen real diamonds before. That pretty lady had really big diamonds on her ears, neck, and on her arm. I just stood there staring at all those diamonds and thinking how much food and nice clothes all those diamonds could buy me and the other kids at the orphanage.

I turned around to grab David by the hand but he was not there. I walked around for a long time just looking for David, but I never did find him, and I never saw him, ever again. Even after they took me back to the orphanage.

I think he walked out into the ocean to find that great big ship and they took him across the ocean where he could be happy. ❖

I T WAS SO HOT ONE NIGHT IN THE ORPHANAGE THAT WE could not sleep. It was almost like someone had thrown a hot, wet blanket over you, and it was very hard to breathe. But that was just part of the problem. One of the boys had dropped the soap sock down the toilet and it had run over and water was all over the bathroom floor. So we all had to clean it up and go to bed without any supper.

I was really hungry and had not eaten anything since breakfast, as I always threw my school lunch away because it was in a brown paper bag, and that was a sign that you were from the orphanage. I tried to hide this fact from any of the new kids at school, hoping for a clean slate with them.

That night, about ten of us boys decided to sneak out of my bedroom window and head out into the unknown world, outside of the orphanage fences. We had heard that they threw away a lot of food at the Morrison's Restaurant Cafeteria over at the South Gate Plaza Shopping Center. So off we headed to hunt for food and drink.

As we walked toward the shopping center we passed this little building called the "Patio Restaurant." It had been closed for several hours but the smell of food coming from the window drew us to it like bees to nectar.

As we walked around the building trying to find out where that delicious smell was coming from, several of the boys were looking through the garbage cans. Dean Whitcomb noticed that the back window was open and called for us to come over. That wonderful smell was being pushed through the back window by a large fan that had been left on in the kitchen.

As we stood in line, taking turns smelling the odor coming from the restaurant, one of the boys leaned against the lower pane of glass and it slid out of its metal case. Of course, it did not take us long to figure out that the other glasses would also slide out. One after the other we removed the glass, carefully placing them beside the back door.

Within minutes all ten of us were inside, eating all the candy that we wanted. We had never eaten like this in our entire lives. It was like being in candy heaven. After we had eaten all that we wanted, we cleaned up after ourselves and went back out through the back window. We replaced the glass and returned to the orphanage for a good night's sleep, with full stomachs.

All day the next day we talked about what we had done. Finding a candy heaven was the greatest thing that could ever happen to us. So it was agreed that we would return every night, eat what we wanted, clean up our mess, and then leave—and no one would be the wiser.

This worked out rather well for the first few days, but then some of the boys talked about taking some of the cigarettes and matches. Most of us were against that because that was really stealing, but eating was okay. I would guess we ended up taking about ten cartons of Parliament, with the recessed filter, which was the first cigarette I ever smoked.

It is unbelievable how a cigarette hanging in the mouth of a young boy could make the girls not notice your big ears. But sooner or later you would run out of cigarettes and your ears seemed to get big again, all of a sudden.

About three weeks later, Wayne Evers and I decided to return to the Patio Restaurant to get another few cartons of cigarettes. When we got to the restaurant I had to help Wayne into the window because he was too small to reach the ledge. After he got in, I climbed into the window and got several cartons of cigarettes and was the first to go back out so that I could help Wayne get back to the ground. I walked over to the bushes to hide the cigarettes and noticed a police car coming around to the back of the restaurant. I lay down in the tall bushes and watched as the policeman walked very slowly up to Wayne and started helping him out of the window. "Don't pull on me, Roger," he yelled out.

The policeman did not say a word but just kept pulling on him.

Wayne started yelling at me again and started trying to kick me because he thought I was pulling on him. Finally, he fell out of the window and landed on his stomach. "You dumb turd," he hollered at me. Then he stood up and noticed the policeman standing there.

I did not see Wayne for about two days. But they finally brought him back to the orphanage after he got out of Juvenile Hall for being a thief. I did give him a few cigarettes out of my two cartons of Parliament. I did not want my ears to go back to being big any sooner than was necessary. ❖

I T WAS AN UNUSUAL FEELING LOOKING BACK AT THE orphanage gates and thinking that we would never have to return there, ever again. Wayne Evers and I had once again decided that we were old enough at the ages of eleven and twelve to take off and start a new life of our own.

It was also a scary feeling leaving the security of the fences of that orphan home. Even as bad as the beatings were, it was still very scary to head out into the unknown world. When ten or fifteen of us orphans would run away out into the darkness together, it was not so bad. But with only two of us, there were just not enough eyes to look and watch out for anything and everything that could come upon us after dark. After all, the orphanage people would be after us, as well as the police, and we knew that there were plenty of bad people out there in the world who would hurt us too.

Once again, having nothing to eat, we decided to drop by the Patio Restaurant and get one last cache of food, candy, and cigarettes to take on our long journey out into the unknown world. It had been several months since Wayne had been caught by the police for illegally entering the Patio

Restaurant, so we were quite sure that it would be safe to enter just one last time, taking only what we really needed to survive until we could each get a job and maybe a place of our own.

When we left the restaurant we had cleaned up our mess and had put all the empty candy wrappers into the garbage can as well as replaced all the glass in the back window. We had taken only what we really needed to survive, which was about fifteen candy bars, ten bags of potato chips, and five cartons of cigarettes each.

We walked over to the old Spanish house, an abandoned house on the south side of Jacksonville, near the orphanage, which was a hideout for any kid who had run away from home, orphan or not. When we arrived we found that there were about ten people staying there, so we headed out to find our own place.

We walked for about two hours and finally decided to try this old, abandoned house that we had heard about over by Landon Junior and Senior High School. It was a very scary looking place. It was a big, two-story white building with almost all the glass broken out of the windows.

We sat outside in the dark for the longest time, talking about the old house and whether the place might have ghosts or not. It sure was a scary-looking old building. But after careful consideration it was decided between our two brilliant minds that there were no such things as ghosts, so we would make this our new home. After all, no one really wanted the old house or they would have taken care of it.

We forced open the front door and we entered the pitch-black house. We lit a match and immediately saw a large staircase to our right. As we started up the stairs they started to creak and we stopped, cold in our tracks, and once again started to think about ghosts and creatures of the night. We stood still for about five minutes just lighting match after match to make sure that there were no ghosts at the top of the stairs.

As we reached the top of the stairs we were about out of matches and our fingers had been burnt from holding the matches for as long as possible.

When we reached the landing at the top of the stairs, it was pitch dark and neither Wayne nor I could even see one another. I took the last match, struck it, and held it high into the air. "There is a bed in here," said Wayne. Just about that time someone large sat straight up in the bed and the darn match went out.

I pushed Wayne toward the staircase and down we went, head first. About that time we heard this large "BANG, BANG," which we found out later was a double-barreled shotgun being fired by the owner of the property. But all we knew right then was that there was a large, ugly ghost sleeping in that bed who was just waiting on us little orphans.

Down the railroad tracks we ran as fast as we could. I was one of the fastest runners in the orphanage, but this time Wayne Evers passed me by and I knew that that darn ghost was going to catch and eat me. By the time we stopped to rest, all our cigarettes, candy bars, and potato chips had been strewn along the two hundred miles of railroad tracks that we ran to get away from that ghost. Well, actually it was about half a mile, but it seemed like two hundred miles.

Late that night we returned to the orphanage and climbed into our warm beds and the orphanage was never the wiser. I think that was the week that I decided to get baptized at the Swain Memorial Methodist Church in Jacksonville. God knows I needed it. ❖

I STAYED UP ALL NIGHT LONG BECAUSE I COULD NOT GO TO sleep. Tomorrow would be my first day of junior high school. It would also be the first time I had ever ventured outside the orphanage by myself, at least in the daytime and never for more than five hundred yards from the fence, legally that is. I had attended Spring Park Elementary School next door to the orphanage for as far back as I could remember. I had always walked to school with all the other orphans who lived in The Children's Association. Other than running away, I had never been outside the fence without the other orphans; it was just too scary. So I was quite worried about what was really outside the fences and in the strange world where all the normal kids lived, the ones who had mothers and fathers and who were always making fun of us kids from the orphanage.

I walked about half a mile to the store where we used to buy candy with our nickel allowance. This was where I was told to go, that it was the only bus stop. I had no idea what I was supposed to do when I got there except get on a yellow bus and ride to Landon Junior and Senior High School. But when I got to the bus stop, there were all kinds of big yellow buses. Buses going this way and buses going that way. Buses going every which way. I was very confused and I started to ask someone what I was supposed to do. Then this very pretty girl made some comment to the other girls about me wearing short pants and why couldn't I button my shirt, which was too small for me. Of course, I still had no choice about the clothes I had to wear.

After the girl made her comment all the other girls started laughing at me. I did not want to look them in the face so I just walked away with my head down and stood behind the edge of the store. I sure wanted to get back to the orphanage awful badly so I could just go to my bedroom and hide so that nobody could look at me or make fun of me.

Within fifteen minutes everyone was gone except for one girl. She looked at me and smiled and then asked what school I was going to attend. I told her "Landon High School." She told me that the Landon bus had already left and that there would be no more buses. I told her that I did not ride the bus, I guess because I was so embarrassed, and that I was waiting for a ride in a car. Finally her bus came and she waved at me as she entered the bus door, turned around, smiled, and told me that she would see me tomorrow. That made me feel really good and now I was not so afraid. I shall always remember that beautiful smile because it was the first time that a girl ever smiled at me. So I saved that smile in a very special place in my mind and I thought about it all day.

There I stood all alone, and now I had no idea what I was going to do. I was totally confused and did not know where to turn or who to turn to. But I knew two things for sure. I knew there was no way out for me and that I was in deep trouble, and I knew that I was going to get a good beating when I returned to the orphanage, just because I missed the yellow bus. So all I could do was just start walking toward the school, which was about ten miles away. God, that was a long, long walk and I guess it was about noontime when I finally arrived at the school. I stood outside the school for about an hour thinking about what I had heard the day before. I heard that the school would also beat you with a wooden paddle if you did something wrong. If they found out that I missed the bus on purpose, then they would beat me with the paddle and then I would get another beating when I got back to the orphanage that afternoon. I dreaded having to walk into that school building with those short pants on. The beating with that wooden paddle was really going to hurt with these short pants on and then all the girls would see the marks on my legs and laugh at me again, just like at the orphanage. But I knew that I did not have a choice. I had to do it today and if not today, then tomorrow. So I might as well get beat today and get it over with.

I know now that there were a lot of children who had the same type of feelings that I had, especially on their first day of school. I guess the thing that bothers me, and the difference between them and me, was the fact that they had someone who loved and cared about them. At least they had a mom and dad who could explain to them that what they were feeling was normal. The orphanage just pushed me out of the gate, leaving me in a strange world, all alone, having no idea what was out there. There I was, just standing there, all alone and scared, thinking the entire time that I was some kind of freak of nature. Just a joke, standing there at the bus stop in my short pants and a shirt that was so small that it would have fit a four-year-old. By the end of the day, when I'd been bused back to the orphanage, you've never seen anyone run so fast to get back inside those fences. It may seem strange, but that's the only world I knew and, in some sense, in which I felt safe. ❖

I WAS SO PROUD THE DAY MY SEVENTH GRADE TEACHER AT Landon Junior High School, Mr. Danpier, agreed to come to the orphanage to eat supper with me. We orphans were absolutely astounded that Mrs. Dalbert would allow us to have our favorite teachers to dinner. It had to be a miracle, because no one had ever entered the orphanage grounds that did not live there or have business at the head office. NO ONE.

Many of the teachers had brought their own children, so after dinner all the orphans and teachers' kids were out in the yard chasing one another around the large grass circle in the center of the orphanage grounds. Finally, out of breath, we all sat down in the grass and were discussing what we wanted to play next. One of the teachers' children yelled out, "Let's play orphan. You two (pointing at Nathan Lawrence and me) can be the mommy and daddy." All of us orphans just looked at him, wondering what the heck he was talking about. One of the little girls jumped up and grabbed Nathan Lawrence by the arm, pulling him to his feet, and told him to stand beside her. "You will be the daddy and I will be the momma," she said. "Now, who is going to be the orphan?" she said, putting her hands up onto her sides, like our matron did when she was disgusted with us. One of the little boys, about three years old, who had been dumped off at the orphanage by his parents just a day or two before, got to his feet and walked slowly toward her. The little girl reached out, turned the little boy around, and placed Nathan Lawrence's arms around the little boy and said "Now, Daddy, you are supposed to hug your little orphan boy." All the teachers' kids started laughing for a long, long time. But none of us orphans laughed at all. We just sat there, being very quiet, just looking at that little boy cry his eyes out, wondering the entire time what the heck was going on and what kind of weird game these strange kids were playing.

After all the teachers and their children had left, we resumed our usual game of Cowboys and Indians, with our bamboo bows and arrows, using Coca-Cola tops bent around the ends as arrowheads.

As I now look back as an adult, I realize what was really happening that day at the orphanage. That poor little boy who had been dropped off at the orphanage by his parents still had a soft, gentle, and loving heart that needed love. He had not yet learned to deal with the loneliness, like the rest of us orphans, by coming to believe that not being hugged, held, or kissed was really no big deal at all, and that it was certainly nothing to cry about. Playing Cowboys and Indians was the only game we really knew and it was all that really counted in our lives. It was a game that could make us feel good about ourselves, and all we wanted was to grow up to be cowboys. ❖

❖ *After* ❖

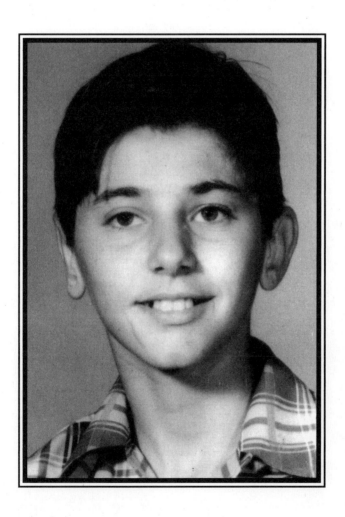

I DIDN'T KNOW IT YET, BUT I HAD WALKED INTO THE mechanical drawing classroom at Landon Junior and Senior High School in Jacksonville, Florida, for the last time. I was sitting at my high desk and had just finished a note that I was going to hand to a girl that I had met several days before. As I was about to hand the note to her, this heavyset bully-type kid grabbed the note from my hands and started unfolding it, saying that he was going to read it before the entire classroom.

I got down from my high stool and walked toward him. The entire classroom was totally silent including the teacher. I stopped in front of him, looked him straight in the eye, and said, "I am going to ask you one time, and one time only, to give me back that note." He laughed and said, "I'm shaking all over." I cold-cocked that bully right between the eyes and then landed a right punch directly in the middle of his fat, bully face, knocking him down onto the floor. Blood from his nose went everywhere—on the drawing tables and all over the students. I reached down and picked the note up off the floor and walked over to the girl that it was intended for and handed it to her. "I am very sorry about this," I told her. I immediately turned around and ran out the classroom door and down the stairs.

When I reached the next landing, a teacher grabbed me by the arm, pulling me to a stop, and said, "Slow down. What's the big hurry?" "Nothing," I told him. Just then the mechanical drawing teacher came running down the stairs and saw the teacher holding my arm. The teacher told him to hold on to me until the principal came and that he was going to call an ambulance, as the mayor's son was laid out, all bloody, on the classroom floor.

I was taken directly to the dean's office, where I was given five swats with the large wooden paddle before they even knew the circumstances of the matter. I was then taken to the principal's office, where he chewed me out for ten or fifteen minutes. I sat very quietly with him asking me over and over, "Do you realize who you hit? That is the mayor's son, George." "I don't really care," I told him. "That fat creep is a big bully and he is no better than anybody else," I said. "You cannot go around hitting the kids of important people," he yelled at me. I stood up and yelled back at him, "Then you tell me why that fat-ass bully is any better than anyone else. I've been beat on all my life and that fat bastard is not going to beat on me or anyone else." Before he could answer, I started to cry and ran out of his office and out of the school and did not stop for what seemed to be miles and miles.

I looked in my pocket and found that I only had twenty-five cents to my name. I knew that I could never return to the orphanage and that I had to get out of Jacksonville, Florida, or I would be beaten to death by the orphanage or sent to prison by the courts for hitting the mayor's bully brat. I just kept walking for miles and miles and had no idea what to do or where I could go. Even though I had run away many times, I always tried to stay in that same neighborhood because I knew my way around and I hid out and slept in abandoned houses and underneath the Spring Park Elementary School building.

I went out onto the main highway leaving Jacksonville and stuck my thumb out, hoping to catch a ride before the police found me. I walked and walked, but no one would stop or offer me a ride. Finally I just gave up and sat down on the side of the road. My legs were sore and my feet were killing me. It was getting colder and colder as the sun started to set behind the clouds. I sat there for about another hour and a big, long black car stopped in front of me.

"Where are you headed?" yelled this woman. "I'm going to California," I yelled back at her. She jumped out of the car and I ran to get into the front seat between her and the man who was driving. "My name is Ethan and this is Mara," he told me. "My name is Roger, and I am headed to California," I said to Ethan. "Well, we are not going that far, but we will give you a lift to Alabama," he said, winking at Mara. We talked and drove for several hours and then Ethan told me that they were going to stop and get a bite to eat. I told them that I was not hungry but that I would sit with them in the restaurant. We entered the restaurant and sat at a booth, where they ordered chicken and fish dinners. God, it smelled so good. My jaws actually hurt from smelling that food, because the muscles in my mouth would move around and make water and all. I had not eaten since that morning at the orphanage and had only eaten one piece of toast because I was late.

Ethan kept looking at me and kept asking me if I was hungry and I kept telling him that I wasn't. I didn't have any money and I was not going to ask anybody for anything. Ethan picked up his salad and shoved it toward me saying, "Eat this damn salad. I'm not going to eat it and it will just go to waste." I ended up eating the salad, two sandwiches, two desserts, and a large drink that they bought me, and God was it good.

After dinner Mara and I walked out to the car and stood beside it, waiting on Ethan to pay for the meal. "How old are you?" she asked me. "How old are you?" I asked her back. "I'm twenty-nine and Ethan is thirty. Now how old are you, young man?" she said. I acted like I did not hear what she said. I did not want them to know my age or they might call the cops and they would take me to prison, or worse, take me back to the orphanage.

A few minutes later Ethan came walking out of the restaurant and told Mara that it was rather late and that maybe they should get a motel room there by the restaurant and then continue to Alabama in the morning. They asked me what I was going to do. I told them that I would just keep hitchhiking on to California. "You can stay in the room with us if you would like," Ethan said. It was really getting cold and I was starting to shiver, so I told him that I would stay and ride with them to Alabama in the morning.

We got up to the room and Mara went and sat on the end of one of the two beds and Ethan sat down in the chair next to me. "What do you think of my wife?" Ethan said. "She is very pretty," I told him. "That's not what I mean," he said. I did not know exactly what he meant, but I started to get a little scared and uneasy because the tone of his voice changed. "I mean how do you like her breasts?" he said to me. I did not know what to say to him. I had looked at her breasts when Ethan went to the bathroom at the restaurant and they looked big in that tight red sweater. But I didn't say anything and I didn't look at them too long.

Ethan got up from his chair and walked over to his wife and raised her sweater and bra over her breasts and up around her neck. I almost stopped breathing, I was so scared. I could not believe that he had shown another man his wife's breasts. Ethan walked over to me and grabbed me by the arm, pulling me out of the chair and toward Mara, who was still sitting on the end of the bed. As I was being pulled toward her, I looked up and she had a great big smile on her face, with real big white teeth and big red lips—lips and teeth that kept getting bigger and bigger, the closer I got to her.

When we got to the end of the bed, Ethan took one of my hands and placed it on one of Mara's large breasts. I just stood there like a statue, not moving a muscle. "How does that feel?" said Ethan. "It feels like that warm jar of tadpoles I had at the orphanage," I said.

"Who wants a drink?" hollered Ethan. "I do, my mouth is really, really dry," I told him. I just stood there with my hand on Mara's big breast, afraid to move or to let go of it. "I'll get us some Coca-Colas," Ethan said, as he dropped his change all over the floor. "Can I go get the Cokes?" I yelled at him, seeing a chance to remove my hand from the large breast without being noticed. "Sure," said Ethan, as he handed me all the change.

I walked out of that motel room door and ran as fast and as far as I could. I hid in the bushes all night long so that Ethan and Mara would not find me if they drove by going to Alabama.

Thank God I knew what a jar of tadpoles felt like or I would have really been up the creek. ❖

AFTER I RAN AWAY FROM MARA AND ETHAN, I MADE MY way back to Jacksonville. At twelve years old I was living on the streets and eating out of dumpsters and garbage cans—but only the ones behind the better restaurants. If you have to be a bum, then you might as well be a high-class bum or there is no point in living anymore.

An old man in the park had given me five dollars for letting him rub on my leg while he did whatever it is they do when they are rubbing a young boy's leg on a dark park bench, late at night.

I had heard from some of the older bums, underneath the train bridge where we slept at night, that the best food to buy was Chinese, as it would not spoil as fast and could be kept for several days. So I walked into this Chinese restaurant to place an order to go. I placed my order and was sitting at one of the booths trying to steal as much sugar, wrapped in napkins, as I could get into my pocket without getting caught. All of a sudden everyone got really quiet when four men came walking into the restaurant, one of them in a policeman's uniform.

It was about three in the morning, so I was really hoping that they would not question me about being so young and why

I was out at such a late hour. They did look at me when they walked by but then continued on down the aisle and turned the corner coming up the other side of the restaurant. I could not believe how quiet it was. There was no sound, whatsoever, not even from the kitchen, which had been clanging pots and pans all around before the four men came walking into the restaurant.

As they made their way down the aisle, they walked very, very slowly, looking at each and every person sitting at the booths. When they passed me, I noticed this girl stick something in her mouth with a fork. All of a sudden one of the men yelled out, "She's got it in her mouth!" The four men jumped on her, forcing her to the floor. One man held her head, another held her legs, and another held her arms. The fourth man started beating her in the face as hard as he could. I could not believe that this was happening. There was blood squirting all over the booth and all the people sitting in the booths next to her. Everyone started yelling and screaming and running all over the place.

I just sat there shaking, too afraid to move. I had not seen anything like this since I left the orphanage. The policeman just kept beating her in the face, over and over, until she opened her mouth and spit out what she had in her mouth. The policeman reached down on the floor and picked it up and then threw it, as hard as he could, down on the table. He looked over at the other men and said, "It's just a f——ing piece of egg roll." "Where are the damn drugs?" yelled the man in plain clothes. "We don't have any drugs, we are from Canada," said the lady. The policeman grabbed her by the hair and started banging her head against the wall. "Where are the GOD DAMN drugs?" he hollered at her. The man that was sitting with the lady jumped up and pushed the man away from her. The policeman grabbed his blackjack and the man sat back down and covered his head.

The policeman slammed his blackjack, as hard as he could, down onto the table and yelled out, "What the hell is everybody looking at?" People started getting out of their booths and walking out of the restaurant. When I stood up to leave, the policeman looked at me and said, "Where the hell are you going?" "To the bathroom—my dad is in there," I said. "Then get your butt in there and don't come out," he told me. I went into the bathroom and locked the door behind me so they couldn't get me. I sat in the corner for hours and didn't open the door, even when people knocked.

I just could not believe that there were people out in the real world that would do this to other people, especially policemen. The orphanage did this kind of stuff to us all the time, but that was because we were orphans and no one cared about us. I knew Officer Topper who walked outside the orphanage fence, and he was real nice. I used to talk with him all the time through the orphanage fence. He would never beat anyone like that. He was a good cop.

Well, I knew right then and there that things were not going to change for the better for me. I didn't know what I was going to do. I had nowhere to go and no one to help me. But I knew that I had to get off the street because the police would beat me too if they caught me.

I was forced to move in with the old man who liked to rub my leg in the park. He was a schoolteacher, and he told me that I could never tell anyone what he did to me, and I never did. ❖

WHEN THE AUTHORITIES FINALLY CAUGHT UP WITH me, I was sent to the Duval County Jail in Jacksonville, Florida. Usually I was sent to Juvenile Hall, but I guess after you've run away five or six times they consider you a career criminal. This was my first introduction into the "adult world" of justice outside of Juvenile Hall and the chain-link fences of the orphanage. It appeared no matter where I went I was always caged up like an animal.

I can't say that I wasn't scared when I entered the jailhouse. Of course, I was always scared when I left the fenced area of the orphanage. I had no idea what was outside of the fence. In jail, downtown, or uptown it was all strange to me.

I was placed in a large cell with about twenty other men who were in their early twenties and thirties. After about an hour, several of the men started fighting with one another. The guards came rushing in and settled the dispute. Then several of the men who were playing cards starting talking about this "young stuff" that had just been brought in. They all were staring and looking at me, and the sex talk and the jokes got quite out of hand. Rather nasty, in fact.

From the tone of the conversation, I suspected what was being planned for me after the lights were turned off. I stole a spoon from a dinner tray and slipped it into my pocket. I went and lay down on my bunk. I carefully bent the spoon handle back and forth until the head of the spoon fell off. I figured the handle would make a good knife.

I had already decided that when these guys went to sleep that I was going to go over to the biggest man and stab him right in the heart with the spoon handle. Finally everyone went to bed. I cannot tell you how afraid I was.

Because of my fear and instinct for self-preservation, at the age of twelve I knew that I might have to take the life of another human being. I shall never forget having to think that thought. It felt like I was called to go to war against the civilian population that I had heard about, living outside the fences of the orphanage. The big guy finally got up and went to the toilet. When he came back, he was shaking his thing at me, laughing, as he passed my bed. I was one scared little boy.

Let there be no doubt in your mind that I would have done whatever was necessary to protect myself. Right then, at the tender age of twelve, I realized once and for all what low sons of bitches human beings could be. That would also be the last time that I would feel that kind of fear. That would be the last time that a tear would enter the eyes of Roger Dean Kiser.

The judge gave up on me just when I needed help the most, and all along I thought judges were really smart people and could see things that other people couldn't. But I guess I was wrong. ❖

FROM THE DUVALL COUNTY JAIL, I WAS SENT TO APPEAR before Judge Davis, who sentenced me to spend the next six years of my life at the Institute for Young Men, Florida at Marianna. I remember that day as if it were yesterday. I remember the hollow sounds of the courtroom doors, the look in the judge's eyes, and the tone of his voice as he shook his head back and forth in disgust.

I was not even afraid as I stood there before him, just looking up at that great big man sitting at that great big table. I did not know what to do, say, or think—I guess because it really did not matter to me anymore because I had already given up on life. Boy, I really could have used my mommy to come and save me that day. I just wanted someone to help me before I disappeared from life just like so many other orphans had done before me.

I hadn't been at the reform school at Marianna for long when they called me to the main office and said that I would soon visit the White House. When I heard this, an unbelievable fear came over me. I swear I almost passed out. I was trembling badly and my legs gave out; I fell to the floor. They told me to get up and sit down on the hard wooden bench outside the office.

I waited there for the two men who would come to take me to the White House. I knew their routine well. I had heard about it from many other boys who had been taken there. Every one of them had been taken against his will.

After a wait of about thirty minutes, the two men came to get me. They grabbed me by my arms and lifted me off the bench. There were several other boys in the office with me, so I had to try to act as though I wasn't scared. But they knew. Everyone knew. The two men walked with me across the grass circle that divided the offices from the White House. We stopped at another office and a man walked out who had only one arm.

He took the place of one of the men who was holding on to me. We then continued walking toward the mess hall. As we rounded the building, I could see "it" right in front of me: "The White House."

My mind was just going crazy with fear. My thoughts seemed to be swimming all around in a circle, like a cat that had been thrown into a cold river. I was just trying to think straight, but words were coming out of my mouth before my mind could think of what it was saying. I was trying to decide if I should run or hide or maybe kill myself; anything was better than what was going to happen to me.

When we reached the door, one of the men took out his keys and stuck one into the lock. I looked back over my shoulder. I saw about fifty other boys looking at me. They just stood quietly, as scared as I was; they didn't say a word. They were just looking and staring at me.

As the White House door opened, an ungodly odor filled my nose. I could hardly breathe. I remember trying to step up into the doorway, but the odor was so overwhelming that I fell into the short hallway inside the door. One of the men grabbed me by the back of the shirt and jerked it up around my neck, choking me. One of the buttons fell off my shirt, hit the floor, and rolled very slowly around the corner. Almost everything was happening in slow motion. My whole body was just numb; it was very difficult for me to breathe. I tried to pull the shirt down from around my neck. But the man jerked my shirt once again and then hit me on the top of the head with his knuckles. He hit me so hard, in fact, that I hit the floor again and bloodied my nose.

At that point, I was not walking; I could not walk. The two men picked me up and carried me into this small room. The room had nothing in it except a bunk bed and a pillow. They put me down and told me to lie on the bed and turn my face toward the wall. I sat on the edge of the bed, crying. I wiped the blood from my nose onto my shirtsleeve.

When I looked up at the men's faces, they were just plain, cold, and hard. Their faces had no expression whatsoever. I did what they told me. One of the men said to move my hands to the top of the bunk bed and to grab the bar at the headboard. I did so.

Not a sound could be heard in the room. Then I felt someone reaching underneath the pillow and pulling something out very slowly. I turned over quickly and looked at one of the men who was standing near my head. He had a large leather strap in his hand. "Turn your damn head back toward the wall," he yelled.

I knew what was going to happen to me, and it was going to be very bad. I had been told what to expect by some of the many boys who had been taken to the White House—others I never heard from again. I had heard that this leather strap was made of two pieces of leather with a line of sheet metal sewn in between the leather halves.

Again, everything was totally silent. I remember tightening my buttocks as tight as I could. Then I waited, and I waited, and I waited. I remember hearing someone take a breath and then a step. I turned over very quickly and looked toward the man who had the leather strap. I remember seeing this ungodly look on his face, and I knew he was going to beat me to death.

I tried to jump off the bed but was knocked backward when the leather strap hit me on the side of the face. The two men grabbed me and held me to the floor. I was yelling to God to save me, begging for someone, anyone, to help me. There was blood all over everything.

"Please forgive me; please forgive me," I kept yelling at the top of my voice. "Please forgive me; dear God, please help me!"

But it did not do any good; not even God heard me that day. Maybe God was smart enough not to ever enter the White House, even to save a child.

After about five minutes of begging, pleading, and crying, they told me to get back onto the bed and grab the top rail again. They warned me that if I tried to get off the bed again, they would start the beating all over again. I slowly pulled myself up off the floor and got back onto the bed. Again I grabbed the rail; again I waited; again everything became quiet, except for the two men breathing really hard.

Once again, I tightened up my buttocks and just waited. Then all of a sudden, it happened. God, I thought my head would explode. The thing came down on me. Over and over it came down on me. I screamed and kicked and yelled as much as I could. But it did not do any good. He just kept beating me. On and on and on. I never let go of that bed rail. Then there was nothing. Just nothing at all.

The next thing I remember, I was sitting on another wooden bench in the one-armed man's office. I remember wiping the slobber and the blood from my mouth. I remember feeling as if my body was on fire. I stood and found that I could hardly stand upright. GOD, GOD, GOD, it hurt so bad! I will never forget that until the day I die.

One of the men in the office yelled at me to sit down. I told him that I had to go to the bathroom. The man pointed at a doorway and said that it was the bathroom and to make it quick.

I slowly walked into the bathroom and closed the door. I looked in the mirror. There was dried blood all over my black-and-blue face, all over my hair, and in my mouth. I took my torn shirt off, which was hanging from the waistband of my pants. I turned around and looked in the mirror and saw that my back was black and blue and bloody.

I started to cry and covered my mouth with both hands, really tight, so that no other boys would hear me. I loosened my belt buckle to get my pants down. It was very painful for me, but the worst was yet to come. As I got my pants down, I noticed that my legs had blood all over them. I stood over the toilet and tried to pee, but it just would not come out.

I decided to take my underwear down and sit on the toilet until I could pee. But the underwear would not come off; it was stuck to my butt and legs. The underwear material had been beaten into the skin of my buttocks, and now it was dried with blood. I pulled my pants back up and washed my face, mainly because I did not want the other boys to see that I had been crying. I couldn't stop shaking.

Finally, I walked back into the outer office and saw Mr. Sealander standing there. He took me back to Cottage Twelve, and he called the office to complain about what had happened to me. Then he took me to the hospital, where the old nurse, Ms. Womack, soaked me in Epsom salts and pulled the underwear from the skin of my buttocks with tweezers.

Why was this done to me? I never knew until years later why I was beaten like that. They did it because I said the word "shit" when I slipped on the diving board at the pool. I don't even remember saying that word. I never was a boy who cursed.

I will never forget being beaten like that without knowing the reason for the beating. I will never forget what adults are capable of doing to a child. I will never forget that the State of Florida was behind what happened to me and to many, many other boys—all for running away from the orphanage.

Thank you, for caring, Mr. Sealander. Wherever you are, I want to thank you for your kindness and understanding. Because of that one deed, as I have grown up, I have learned to trust, respect, and take the word of my fellow man. I will always remember, respect, and love you for that. ❖

I WAS THIRTEEN YEARS OLD AND WAS LIVING ON MY OWN IN a rooming house on Forsythe Street in Jacksonville, Florida. I was there because I would not return to the abusive orphanage that I had been raised in and the juvenile court did not want to send me back to the reform school. So the juvenile judge allowed me, under supervision, to get a job at a sheet metal shop and live at the rooming house, which was about a block from the juvenile court building.

I had gotten the name "Gavin Gamble" from someone associated with an air force military magazine subscription, and the name was supposed to have something to do with my natural mother. One day after work I decided to sit down at the rooming house telephone and call every city in the United States to see if there was a Gavin Gamble listed in their city or town. I made a long list of every major city in the United States, and then started calling directory assistance information in every state, starting with the states that had the fewest amount of major cities in them. Within several hours I had reached an operator who found the name of a Gavin Gamble, living at 127 President Drive, in Dover, Delaware. I asked the woman at the rooming house if I could call the number and she agreed, as long as I would pay her for the telephone call when I got my pay. I dialed the number, very nervously, and heard a woman's voice answer, "Hello?" "Is this Mrs. Gamble?" I asked her. "Yes it is, and who is this?" she said. "This is Roger. Are you my mother?" I asked her. "Who?" she said again. "Roger Dean Kiser," I told her. "How did you get my number?" she said. "I got it from the operator," I replied. "I cannot talk right now, can I telephone you back later? Give me your number," she said to me. I gave her the number of the rooming house and hung up. I was so excited that I had heard my mother's voice for the first time I could remember. That was a wonderful feeling and I told everyone I knew about it. But she never called me back, even though I waited by that black telephone every hour that I was not working.

I worked real hard for about a month, eating only one ten-cent Krystal hamburger every day, and I saved enough money to buy a Greyhound bus ticket and go and live with my mother, where I belonged. So off I headed from Jacksonville, Florida, to Dover, Delaware.

I arrived in Dover, Delaware, at around 9:00 a.m. and was shocked to see snow all over the ground. I had never seen snow before and did not realize how cold it was, and I was shaking all over after I got off the bus. But that was okay. I would soon be in the arms of my mother for the first time in my life and she would make me warm and take care of me and I would never have to be afraid, ever again. I walked up to the post office, where I saw a pay phone, and pulled out that wonderful number that I had been given by the information operator. I dialed the number and once again I heard the beautiful voice of my mother. "Hello?" she said. "Mom, this is Roger," I said softly into the telephone. "Where are you?" she asked. "I am at the post office," I said. "What post office are you at?" she asked. "The post office here in Dover," I told her. Things were perfectly quiet for about thirty seconds. "What are you doing here?" she asked me. "I've come home, Mom," I told her. There was another long silence and then she said, "You wait there. I will be there in a few minutes," and she hung up.

I stood there cold and shaking in the light wind, trying to stand behind those great big white pillars of the post office building. I was watching and looking at each and every woman who walked by or came near me, wondering if that was the one who was my mother. I was very excited but something deep inside of me kept telling me that something was not right here. But I really did not care. My mother was coming to take me home and everything was going to be all right, you'll see, I told myself. I guess I waited about half an hour and all of a sudden I heard a car horn honking. I looked all around but did not see anything. Finally, I noticed a woman parked out on the street, in a station wagon, waving at me. I picked up my very large brown suitcase and walked toward the vehicle. I opened the front door and she told me to put my suitcase in the back seat, which I did. Then I got into the front seat with her and just sat there real still. "How are you?" she asked me. "I am fine, Mom," I said. Nothing more was said until after we had reached her home, and we never even looked one another in the eye, the entire time.

As we entered the house I noticed beer cans sitting everywhere. There had to be hundreds of them all over the place. I sat down in a chair in the living room and noticed a woman sitting at the kitchen table. There were also three or four young children running all around the house like crazy people. The woman got up and walked into the living room and introduced herself as Emily Kent. I said, "Hi," shook her hand, and then sat very quietly, not saying a word to anyone. About an hour later the front door opened and in walked this very tall man in air force work clothing. My mother jumped up rather quickly, grabbed him by the arm, and hurried him down the hallway, toward the back of the house. I noticed that Emily Kent kept looking at me once in a while, smiling rather kindly, as though she knew something that I didn't. But I just could not figure out what it was. The tall man finally walked back down the hallway and into the living room, walked over to where I was sitting, stood in front of me, held out his hand and said, "Hi, my name is Gavin and I am very glad to meet you, Roger." I shook his hand but was afraid to do anything except say, "Thank you, sir."

Gavin was very kind and considerate toward me over the next week or so, and we discussed me working for him one day at his gas station/garage that he had in Dover. It was also decided that I would have to return to school to get an education as I had only completed the sixth grade before dropping out of school and being sent to the reform school in Marianna.

My first day of school in Dover, Delaware, ended up being my last day because I got into a fight with another boy in the gym for calling me a big-eared bastard. When I returned to my mother's home she was furious at me and started yelling at the top of her voice. Then she walked over to the counter and threw a letter at me that I had written and mailed in her mailbox several days before to a friend of mine in Jacksonville. "What is this f——in' s——t," she yelled at me, as loud as she could, pointing to the letter. I was very embarrassed when I saw that paper lying on the floor, because I knew what I had written in the letter and that I should not have written it. In the letter, written to a teenage male friend of mine in Florida, I had written the following message: "I love it here and I am very happy for the first time in my life. There are lots of girls all over the place and I am getting lots of p——y.—Roger"

Well, I was so ashamed of myself and so embarrassed that I did not know how to react. I had written this letter partly because of my age, wanting to be looked upon as a man, and partly because of what I had seen happening around my mother's house. Sex between she and Gavin was an everyday occurrence. I had passed their bedroom many times, with their door ajar, and I knew what was happening because of the type of sounds coming from their room, as did the younger children in that household.

My mother just kept on yelling and screaming and it went on, and on, and on for more than an hour. Finally I got up, walked into my bedroom, took my suitcase out of the closet, and started packing it with what few clothes I had. "Where are you going?" said my mother. "I'm going back to Florida, where I belong," I told her. "Just as well," she said, as she turned around, walked away, and slammed the door. I finished packing my large suitcase and walked out her front door, without saying a word, and I never looked back. I walked for miles and miles in the snow, crying my eyes out and shivering from the cold. I have never in my entire life ever known a more lonely moment than at that very instant. Now I had no mother, not even an orphanage, to look out for me. I was now, without a doubt, truly all alone in the world.

Eventually, the police stopped me and asked me where I was going with such a big, heavy suitcase. I told them that I was heading to Florida to try and see if the orphanage would take me back. The policeman just smiled, rubbed me on the head, and told me to get into the back of his police car, and he took me to the police station. I was placed in a small cell and told to wait. I opened my big, brown suitcase and took all my clothes out, laying them against the iron wall all in a row. I then took my folded pants and laid them on the iron bed, as there was no mattress, and made a soft bed. I then climbed on and immediately fell asleep. When I was awakened by a policeman, I noticed the lady that I had seen the first day I came to my mother's house standing outside the bars, smiling at me. "Would you like to come and live with me?" she said. "I guess," I told her. "You can baby-sit for me and my husband and I will see that you get a bus ticket back to Florida," she stated.

I stayed with them and baby-sat for about a month or so and was then given some money and a bus ticket back to Florida. While I was staying at Mrs. Kent's house, she was always very kind, gentle, and sweet to me. While I was there my mother came to her house five or six times to have coffee, but she never did speak to me, ever again. I think I remember her coming to the bus station when I left Delaware, but I don't really remember if anything was said or what actually happened because it was just too sad for me. I had finally come to the conclusion that I really was an orphan—for good. ❖

AFTER MY TRIP TO DELAWARE, I WAS LOCKED UP IN Juvenile Hall again because I had left my job and I refused to return to The Children's Association. I was not going to return to that orphanage even if I had to spend the rest of my life locked up in a small cell. I had been at Juvenile Hall for several weeks and refused to even walk out of the front door to help clean up the streets for fear that they would trick me and take me back to the orphanage. I was taking no chances whatsoever.

It was a Wednesday morning. Bert, an attendant who worked at the Juvenile Hall, came into my cell and asked me if I wanted to go somewhere for a Thanksgiving dinner. I told him that I did not want to go outside of the Hall and that he knew why. I liked Bert because he seemed like a nice guy, and besides, his brother had made a song that was played on the radio called "The Lion Sleeps Tonight." I was really impressed by that. But he kept on and on about the Thanksgiving dinner, so I finally said that I would go. Later that day a woman named Mrs. Usher came and talked with me and told me that she wanted to take me to her house for dinner and she promised me that she would bring me back the day after Thanksgiving.

She and I walked out of Juvenile Hall together and drove to her house. It was a nice house, too, and right in the middle of where the rich folks lived, next to the big river with the great big bridge. I had never been over that bridge before because it was just too big to cross. Even when we ran away from the orphanage, we only crossed the little bridges.

We walked into her house and I was really surprised at what I saw. It was real small inside, not like the big houses I had lived in. You could sleep thirty or forty people in our house at the orphanage. Then I went to their bathroom and I saw right away that they were not rich at all. They only had one toilet and one sink in their bathroom! They were really poor and they did not even know it.

As you can gather, other than the brief stay at my mother's and the Kents' (for which most of the time I'd been in a fog), I had never been in a regular house before. I didn't even know that regular people only had one toilet and one sink in their bathrooms.

This ordeal of having to adjust to the "normal" world was very hard on me and I wanted to get out of there very badly. There must have been fifty people in and out of their house getting ready for this big Thanksgiving Day dinner. I was really scared and could not move an inch in any direction and would not move from the chair in which I was sitting in their living room. Mrs. Usher came in and asked me if I wanted a Coke in the small bottle and I told her thank you but that I did not want anything.

I really wanted that Coke, but I was too scared to take it. I thought about that Coke all day long and how good it would have tasted. Later that night I went into the kitchen and took one out of the refrigerator after everyone was asleep. I drank it real fast and hid the bottle cap behind the refrigerator and put the bottle in the case where no one would know I had drunk it. No one would ever know that I had that Coke.

The next day was almost unbearable for me because there were so many strangers coming for dinner at their house. I felt like I would rather have died than have to go through such a horrible experience. I felt awkward and embarrassed and unable to talk with anyone. I hardly ate anything that day and I had never seen so much food in all my life. I was so glad when it was over.

That night Mrs. Usher took me out onto her front porch and we talked for hours. She was a very nice woman and she let me smoke a cigarette because I liked to smoke and it made me feel like I could take care of myself. I think I was thirteen years old at that time, and I had never just sat and talked with anyone before in peace. It was my first "nice and slow time," and I liked doing that. I will never forget that day nor her kindness. But I could not understand why she was doing all of this for me, so I always kept one wary eye on her the whole time. After a while, Mrs. Usher got up and went into the kitchen and brought us both a small Coke in the bottle and handed one to me. Without having to sneak and amidst my newfound peace on her porch, that was the best Coke I ever drank.

The next morning she and I ate some breakfast together and then she told me to go into the bedroom and get my things together so we could go back to Juvenile Hall. I remember going into the bedroom and closing the door. I heard her in the hallway talking on the telephone to the authorities. I heard her ask them why I was being sent back to the reform school and what it was that I had done to be sent back there. They told her that I had done nothing wrong but that they had nowhere else to put me.

I heard her get mad at them and tell them that she was not going to bring me back to be locked up again like a dog. GOD, I LOVED THAT WOMAN FOR SAYING THAT. That is the most wonderful thing anyone ever did for me as a child. That, of all the things in my life, is the one thing that made me want to be somebody, and I thank you so much, you loving, kind, and wonderful woman. That one little sentence that came out of her mouth was the one small light that guided my life for the next forty-five years.

I stayed there with the Ushers for several weeks, and then I left to go out on my own at the age of fourteen. I continued to see the Usher family on and off for the next twenty or thirty years until their deaths. I know that they would have adopted me if I had asked. But, when it was discussed, I told Mrs. Usher that it was too late for me and she cried. I told her that I had to make it on my own. I just wish that I could have shown them how much I really loved them before they died. But I didn't know how to show them that, and I hope that now that they are in heaven that they know how much I love and respect them in my heart.

I LOVE YOU, Mom and Dad Usher. ❖

EPILOGUE

DURING THE COURSE OF WRITING THIS BOOK, I encountered many people from my sorrowful past, some of whom were quite willing to discuss their role in my youth. It was a healing experience for me, for the most part, to see that the conditions for orphaned children have progressed over the years. Still, I fear that abuse may be lurking in places where no one is looking, and so I feel these stories must be told over and over to remind people to keep a watchful eye.

After organizing a reunion of orphaned children in Jacksonville, Florida, in 1991, I learned that Mrs. Douglas, one of my former house parents from The Children's Association, was living in Asheville, North Carolina. Several weeks later, I drove up to see her, and we visited and talked for several hours. As I was about to leave, she asked me to come down to her basement and help her get something important. So we climbed down into her dark, damp cellar. This shaking, seventy-five-year-old woman walked over into a dark corner and picked something up. As she turned around, I could see that she was holding a little table with four broken legs.

"Do you remember this?" she asked.

I just stood there with my head down, and I did not say a word. I could not speak for fear of crying. "Roger, I want you to have this."

Mrs. Douglas gave me back the table that so long ago I had given up for lost and discarded. She had kept it all these years, not knowing if she would ever see me again. Her intention was to save the table because she could not rid herself of the pain she remembered seeing in this orphan's eyes. My name was still etched on the underside of the table. Since then, I have sanded, clear-coated, and replaced the legs. That little Formica table— my first woodworking project from so many years ago—now sits in my granddaughter Chelsey's bedroom, along with her little plastic chair that her papa gave her. I look at that table today with bittersweet memories. I think of my heartbreak and disappointment when Mrs. Dalbert forced me to throw my table that she'd destroyed out the door. But I am comforted and rejoice at the kindness of Mrs. Douglas, who kept that little table as a remembrance—never wanting to forget the story of a young orphan who tried so very hard to please. Thank you, Mrs. Douglas.

I also found Russell Wagner, one of the boys who suffered through the "arena" beatings at the orphanage with me. He spoke with me on the telephone on March 6, 1999, from his home in Clermont, Georgia. We were discussing this book project and certain incidents that happened while we were in the orphanage together. When I told him that I was writing about the "arena beatings," he went completely to pieces, which prompted me to cry as well. There are tears in my eyes still as I think about what happened to Russell the time he was beaten on the side of his head with a croquet mallet, his face and head swollen like a beach ball, and the skin torn away from his forehead. Russell, like myself, surely was a mess for a long, long time.

I was also fortunate enough to encounter Mrs. Harrell, the teacher who helped call attention to the abuse that I experienced at the hands of my stepgrandparents. Mrs. Harrell recounted her memories to me in a September 30, 1999, letter:

Dear Roger,

After talking with you I remembered that my sister-in-law Margaret to whom you talked to get my address is the historian of Dixieland School. She has a lot of pictures, since she was also the photographer. I bet she has a picture of the merry-go-round.

I will never forget my first interview with Mrs. Avery. We teachers came to school two weeks early so we could be ready to get going on the first day of school.

As soon as I got my list of pupils, I called all the parents and set up a time for each one to talk with me about the child who would be in my care. Sometimes both father and mother came and most of them were totally interested.

Mrs. Avery was something else again. She always wore black or dark brown, and she was a very large woman. Before I could get my own mouth open, she started right in and gave me your history of desertion by first your father and then your mother, managing to make it seem to be your own fault. She did not care to listen to anything I had to say, finishing with a flourish of "he's retarded anyway, you don't need to teach him, just certify that he's mentally deficient and we'll put him in the State School!"

The minute she left, I trotted down the hall to Mrs. Silks, the principal. She heard it before I did! She didn't seem as appalled as I was.

It was later when I heard Mrs. Bradford, the sixth grade teacher, say that Mrs. Silks hadn't believed any of it.

I knew when I looked at you, that she was very off track and just trying to get rid of you. We took those I.Q. tests the first week of school and then I knew I was right.

You had about six weeks with me. How you did love school! And then when you learned to read in six weeks, and took home the book to read, all hell broke loose. I thought maybe Mrs. A. would see that she was wrong also.

That was a long two weeks waiting to get the Juvenile Authority after her. I had to go with him because I made the complaint; I was frankly scared of her myself. In this day and time she would have probably shot me!

I'm glad I saved your life, but I wish it had been a better one. At least you knew that one person loved you and cared what happened. You must be a very strong person to have survived!

Sincerely, with love,
Grace Lane Harrell

Since the abuse that I and other orphans suffered came at the hands of the State of Florida, I felt compelled to follow up with the state on their practices. I was relieved to receive correspondence that confirmed that corrective steps have been taken in these institutions, and I was also finally relieved of the burden of carrying this information for so many years. The following letters provided me with some form of closure:

Letter from the Office of the Governor of Florida, Dated May 6, 1999

Dear Mr. Kiser,

I do not know what to say to your message (story). It is a heartfelt, painful, incredible story. I am so sorry.

I will ask our Secretaries of DJJ and DCF to review their agencies and respond to you directly about current policies, as you have requested that we look into current practices. I hope and pray that nothing like this ever happens in Florida today.

Thank you for your message. I will forward your letter along with this response to the Governor. I hope you are doing okay now.

David Rancourt

Letter from Judge Kathleen A. Kearney, Dated August 20, 1999

Dear Mr. Kiser:

Governor Bush has asked that I respond to you on his behalf.

I am sorry to hear of the experiences you had during the time you spent in the Institute for Young Men, Florida. This Department did not exist when you were there. However, I am told that the "white house" and corporal punishment were banned in the institutions around 1967. I am pleased to say that children do not have to endure that kind of experience today. Now, a 24-hour abuse hotline is available to everyone, and state law requires that specified state employees report any abuse or neglect that they observe.

The former training school now houses the Dozier School and is part of the Department of Juvenile Justice. At the Dozier School, the children have free access to a telephone, and they can report abuse that occurs.

This Department and the Office of Inspector General for the Department of Juvenile Justice investigate all such reports.

Good luck in your future endeavors,

Very truly yours,
Judge Kathleen A. Kearney

I WISH TO TAKE THIS TIME TO THANK THE INDIVIDUALS, whomever they are, who had the heart, compassion, and guts to stop such evil deeds committed by the State of Florida.

Although many people have been receptive during my quest to resolve the past, not all have been so open. My mother, for instance, has never been willing to acknowledge me as her son. To this day, I have never figured out why our mother has not wanted to have contact with my sister and me as adults. She lives less than three hundred miles from my home in Georgia. I had always thought that she refused me because she did not want her new family to know about her past life, which I can understand. In fact, in the one meeting I did have with her in 1982 at a restaurant in Rome, Georgia, we agreed that her past need not be revealed.

While I can understand her not wanting to see me, I cannot understand why she has never written or even sent me a Christmas card. There has never been any type of acknowledgment from her that I exist on the face of this earth—or that she has any grandchildren or great-grandchildren by me. In fact, if

I were to run into her in person, I would be just another man in his fifties walking down the street.

My mother had a very hard life; there is no doubt about that. She was adopted, and she was treated very badly by that family, as if she were a possession rather than a child. However, many of the terrible things that happened to Patricia when she became older were the result of her own doing, not of her being adopted or mistreated. The terrible things that happened to Patricia's own children were caused by the decisions that she herself made. Yet she seems to have chosen to hold her children responsible for whatever bad things happened to her in the past.

I guess my mother must be in her seventies by now. She has many wonderful grandchildren and great-grandchildren, all of whom she will never have the opportunity to know. Will my mother ever realize that the past never goes away? Even long after she is gone, the past will still be there, and her grandchildren will remember her not because of what she did to Linda or me but because of what she did to them, because she was not there for them. How much we could have eased your sorrow, Mother, had you only given us a chance! Now we all must live in sorrow. What a pity.

In spite of all that happened to me, I never became hard or cruel. I have always tried to help my fellow human being. Somewhere inside of me I still have an overriding compassion for humankind as a whole. Perhaps, it was the few small acts of kindness that were shown to me that made the difference—the volunteers that took us on a trip here or there, just to catch a glimpse of the real world. That is why it is so important for organizations and clubs, such as the Shriners, Masons, and

Jaycees, to continue to reach out and help children. My memory of these experiences helped to carry me through in times of despair. It is these tiny acts of kindness (though not love) that may keep one confused child from going off the deep end one day. That small glimmer of kindness that was shown by someone, that little speck of hope, will forever remain to be called upon in times of need. It is with this in mind that I say thank you to the people of my past for the few acts of kindness I received, which I now share with my children and grandchildren fifty years later.

In conclusion, I must say that even as a child, I knew how things were supposed to be. I knew that humans should care for one another. Not letting go of that conviction is no doubt what saved me in the end.